Discussions of the Canterbury Tales

DISCUSSIONS OF LITERATURE

General Editor JOSEPH H. SUMMERS, Washington University

Edited by

The *Canterbury Tales*	CHARLES A. OWEN, JR., University of Connecticut
Hamlet	J. C. LEVENSON, University of Minnesota
Alexander Pope	RUFUS A. BLANSHARD, University of Connecticut
The Novel	ROGER SALE, Amherst College
George Eliot	RICHARD STANG, Carleton College
Moby-Dick	MILTON R. STERN, University of Connecticut

DISCUSSIONS

OF THE

CANTERBURY TALES

Edited with an Introduction by

Charles A. Owen, Jr.

THE UNIVERSITY OF CONNECTICUT

D. C. Heath and Company

BOSTON

CONTENTS

Contents

IV. General

INTRODUCTION

MANY things in Chaucer make an immediate appeal. He understood for instance what spring means to people, their desire to get away from the humdrum routine when winter breaks under the impact of the gentle west wind and nature comes alive again. So he started his pilgrims on their way to Canterbury in mid-April, joined them himself, took note of their behavior and the stories they told to amuse and enlighten one another, and wrote it all down in a style as colloquial as Hemingway's and far less self-conscious. It was the happiest inspiration of his career, this pilgrimage; it lasted till his death in 1400; and as he aged physically his pilgrims kept surprising him—they drew from him more and more of his memories of men, of books, of affairs. He was never younger than while he was under their influence, though he was well past forty when he first came under it.

The *Canterbury Tales* is unique. No other work so fragmentary creates such an illusion of completeness. The secret lies perhaps in what Milton Miller calls Chaucer's position of centrality, a position not only social, moral, and philosophical, but, in his final work, literary as well. For Chaucer is *there*, not just as the poet telling an ancient story, as in the *Troilus* and the *Legend of Good Women*, but as the pilgrim whose experiences provide the poet with his material. The centrality is more than a physical presence. It is an attitude as well. The poet *excludes* nothing from his account. As a result we miss less than we would otherwise the three-quarters he didn't live to create. In fact we are hardly aware of it.

Though the poet speaks to us directly of his own experience, his directness and the general ease of his manner are the opposite of simple artlessness. Chaucer attained to them fully only in his old age and in the maturity of his art. But the simplicity with which he speaks in the *Canterbury Tales* helps to explain the many generations who misconceived what they read, who thought of Chaucer as an untutored genius speaking to an uncouth age. We know now, thanks to the effort of scholars over the past hundred years, how false an image that was. We know the extent of his borrowing, of his dependence on other books, in what seemed most direct. We have a reasonably accurate text to read and some knowledge of fourteenth-century pronunciation; hence we are more aware of his skill as a metrist. We have a firmer knowledge of the chronology of his works and can see the extent to which the simplicity and directness rest on a long training in his art as well as on native genius. But we are only beginning to carry on the kind of critical discussion of the *Canterbury Tales* that since Dryden we have conducted of *Hamlet*.

The essays in this book are a selection from this beginning. They represent a challenge and an invitation, rather than a set of firm conclusions. Their aim is to challenge the many new readers of Chaucer to a more sensitive reading of his poetry, and at the same time to invite them to join the discussion. The discussion presents some special obstacles and inducements. The very distance in time and the difference in "climates of opinion," though they make more difficult a complete understanding, also make discovery more exciting—the discovery Dryden made before us that "nothing [is] lost out of nature, tho' everything is alter'd."

The first part of the collection is chronological. It brings together the references to Chaucer that have become a part of the awareness of English-speaking people, even of those who have never read Chaucer's own verses. Each of them is by a poet acutely conscious of his own position in a literary tradition and qualified to appreciate the fellow-poet who sent his *Troilus* into the world with the admonition,

> Go, litel bok, go, litel myn tragedye,
> Ther God thi makere yet, er that he dye,
> So sende myght to make in som comedye!
> But litel bok, no makyng thow n'envie,
> But subgit be to alle poesye;
> And kis the steppes, where as thow seest pace
> Virgile, Ovide, Omer, Lucan, and Stace.

Spenser, Milton, Dryden, Coleridge, and Arnold suggest the continuous appeal of Chaucer. In *Il Penseroso* Milton startles us into a new appreciation by the exalted company in which he places him: it is as if Milton anticipated, and disagreed with, Arnold's refusal to find in Chaucer "high seriousness." Dryden and Arnold raise other important critical issues, Dryden with his emphasis on the general and continuing truth of Chaucer's characterization, Arnold by his effort to define the appeal of Chaucer's poetry.

The last three sections divide the current discussion somewhat arbitrarily according to subject-matter. In the first, on the *Prologue* and frame of the *Canterbury Tales*, we find Hoffman's brilliant treatment of the interaction between theme and structure in the portraits of the *Prologue;* Donaldson's and Malone's consideration of the two figures most certain to have had historical counterparts, namely Chaucer himself and the Host; Baldwin's analysis of the handling of space and time in the *Prologue* with thematic implications for the whole work; and Kittredge's influential view of the tales as dramatic utterances of the pilgrims. The essays of Donaldson and Malone are written specifically in answer to other comment on the *Canterbury Tales*. But all five take issue with the idea of Chaucer as an unsophisticated realist who created his pilgrimage from a journalistic observation of what he saw around him.

The complementary and overlapping aims of the last two groups of essays are to present differing approaches to each of the most famous of the tales, to provide stimulating criticism of the major genres, to suggest an image of the poet against the aesthetic and intellectual background of the late Middle Ages, and to bring him into relationship with the world of letters in which he thought of himself as living. The study of the tales opens with Dale Underwood's essay on the *Knight's Tale*, surveying the many previous articles and enhancing our appreciation of the Boethian influence so apparent in individual passages of the poem. Here the study of a source illuminates the history of ideas and shows Chaucer's relation with one of the germinal forces in Western thought for over a thousand years. Tillyard's brilliant consideration of plot in the *Miller's Tale* was the first serious analysis of one of Chaucer's bawdy tales, and it proves what rewards an unembarrassed study of such a tale can bring. Raymond Preston, dealing with the tales of the Man of Law and the Clerk, joins Arnold in trying to define the quality of Chaucer's poetry.

Charles Muscatine in his consideration of the *Nun's Priest's Tale* against the background of the French tradition shows what a delicate instrument stylistic analysis can be, what a protection against oversimplification, and what an illumination of Chaucer's most complex and sophisticated story. His discussion of Chaucer and the fifteenth century is, like Preston's "Epilogue," a pioneering effort. Wayne Shumaker takes direct aim at the implicit target of both Muscatine and Preston, the "cliché" of Chaucer's modernity. From a well-reasoned study of what we don't find, as well as what we do, in the Wife of Bath's confession he draws stimulating conclusions on Chaucer's aims as a poet and the reasons for his success. John Speirs's introduction on the *Canterbury Tales* serves somewhat to redress the balance, for he places emphasis on what was new in Chaucer's art, especially on the "dramatic-poetic development of English speech."

Most of the essays in the section on the tales have already pointed the way to the final group. Here Milton Miller first takes up the issue of "high seriousness," showing the influence of Christianity on the classical concepts of comedy, tragedy, and fate and defending Chaucer from Arnold's strictures; he then carries off that most difficult of critical ventures, an extended definition by comparison, using the *Nun's Priest's Tale* and Lawrence's *The Man Who Died* as his texts. Bertrand Bronson gives a carefully measured consideration to Chaucer's audience and concludes that we owe a great deal to their sensitive perception of Chaucer's humor and irony. With Morton Bloomfield we come to consider Chaucer's own sense of history, the extent to which it was unusual in his day, and the part it played in his poetry. Finally John Livingston Lowes makes some refreshing observations. His comments on Chaucer's skill in characterization, on the combination of learning and experience in his work, on the quality of his poetry full of concrete detail and instinct with the accent of living speech, create an image of Chaucer's achievement as poet.

The emphasis on Chaucer's poetry is the right one to end with, for we are too apt to think of him as simply a storyteller. The translations of Chaucer, as both Lowes and Arnold point out, hardly do him justice. If we would really know him, we must read him in his own idiom. Paradoxically the language creates less difficulty today than at any time since the early sixteenth century. Chaucer is understood and appreciated more widely by our generation than by any of our forebears. People are discovering that behind the slight barriers of his Middle English language and his medieval world there are values well worth the seeking. This collection will serve its purpose if it can help in removing the barriers and in indicating the values, if it can send some readers back to the *Canterbury Tales* with an enlightened interest and an awareness of the pleasures to be derived from a second reading, if it can suggest the art of his apparent simplicity and encourage others to explore it further. Chaucer's comedy combines a keen criticism of the society he observed with a quiet assurance of manner and an extraordinary zest for life. Seldom has an artist been so unobtrusive—or so successful in creating a convincing world in his art.

CHARLES A. OWEN, JR.

Discussions of the Canterbury Tales

DISCUSSIONS OF LITERATURE

The *Canterbury Tales*

Edmund Spenser

from The Faerie Queene

BOOK IV, CANTO II [1]

XXXII

Whylome, as antique stories tellen us,
Those two [2] were foes the fellonest on ground,
And battell made the dreddest daungerous
That ever shrilling trumpet did resound;
Though now their acts be no where to be found,
As that renowmed poet them compyled
With warlike numbers and heroicke sound,
Dan Chaucer, well of English undefyled,
On Fames eternall beadroll worthie to be fyled.

XXXIII

But wicked Time, that all good thoughts doth waste,
And workes of noblest wits to nought out weare,
That famous moniment hath quite defaste,
And robd the world of threasure endlesse deare,
The which mote have enriched all us heare.
O cursed Eld, the cankerworme of writs!
How may these rimes, so rude as doth appeare,
Hope to endure, sith workes of heavenly wits
Are quite devourd, and brought to nought by little bits?

---

[1] From *The Second Part of the Faerie Queene,* first published in 1596.
[2] "Couragious Cambell, and stout Triamond," whose fierce battle over Canacee
serves as climax to Spenser's continuation of the *Squire's Tale.*

XXXIV

Then pardon, O most sacred happie spirit,
That I thy labours lost may thus revive,
And steale from thee the meede of thy due merit,
That none durst ever whilest thou wast alive,
And, being dead, in vaine yet many strive:
Ne dare I like, but through infusion sweete
Of thine owne spirit, which doth in me survive,
I follow here the footing of thy feete,
That with thy meaning so I may the rather meete.

John Milton

from Il Penseroso[1]

But, O sad Virgin, that thy power
Might raise *Musaeus* from his bower,
Or bid the soul of *Orpheus* sing
Such notes as warbled to the string,
Drew Iron tears down *Pluto's* cheek,
And made Hell grant what love did seek.
Or call up him that left half told
The story of *Cambuscan* bold,
Of *Camball* and of *Algarsife*,
And who had *Canace* to wife,
That own'd the virtuous Ring and Glass,
And of the wondrous Hors of Brass,
On which the *Tartar* King did ride;
And if ought els, great *Bards* beside,
In sage and solemn tunes have sung,
Of Turneys and of Trophies hung;
Of Forests, and inchantments drear,
Where more is meant then meets the ear.
                              [Lines 103–120]

---

1 Written 1632; published 1645.

John Dryden

from Preface to the Fables [1]

IT REMAINS that I say something of Chaucer in particular.

In the first place, as he is the father of English poetry, so I hold him in the same degree of veneration as the Grecians held Homer or the Romans Virgil. He is a perpetual fountain of good sense, learn'd in all sciences, and therefore speaks properly on all subjects: as he knew what to say, so he knows also when to leave off, a continence which is practic'd by few writers, and scarcely by any of the ancients, excepting Virgil and Horace. . . .

. . . He must have been a man of a most wonderful comprehensive nature, because, as it has been truly observ'd of him, he has taken into the compass of his *Canterbury Tales* the various manners and humors (as we now call them) of the whole English nation, in his age. Not a single character has escap'd him. All his pilgrims are severally distinguish'd from each other; and not only in their inclinations, but in their very physiognomies and persons. Baptista Porta [2] could not have describ'd their natures better, than by the marks which the poet gives them. The matter and manner of their tales, and of their telling, are so suited to their different educations, humors, and callings, that each of them would be improper in any other mouth. Even the grave and serious characters are distinguish'd by their several sorts of gravity: their discourses are such as belong to their age, their calling, and their breeding; such as are becoming of them, and of them only. Some of his persons are vicious, and some virtuous; some are unlearn'd, or (as Chaucer calls them) lewd, and some are learn'd. Even the ribaldry of the low characters is different: the Reeve, the Miller, and the Cook are several men, and distinguish'd from each other, as much as the mincing Lady Prioress and the broad-speaking gaptooth'd Wife of Bath. But enough of this: there is such a variety of game springing up before me, that I am distracted in my choice, and know not which to follow. 'Tis sufficient to say, according to the proverb, that here is God's plenty. We have our forefathers and great-grandames all before us, as they were in Chaucer's days; their general characters are still remaining in mankind, and even in England, tho' they are called by other names than those of Monks and Friars, and Canons, and Lady Abbesses, and Nuns: for mankind is ever the same, and nothing lost out of nature, tho' everything is alter'd.

[1] *Fables, Ancient and Modern*, published in 1700 within two months of Dryden's death, included his versions of *The Knight's Tale, The Nun's Priest's Tale*, and *The Wife of Bath's Tale*.

[2] Neapolitan physician, author of *De Humana Physiognomia*, 1586.

Samuel Taylor Coleridge

from Table Talk [1]

March 15, 1834

I TAKE unceasing delight in Chaucer. His manly cheerfulness is especially delicious to me in my old age. How exquisitely tender he is, and yet how perfectly free from the least touch of sickly melancholy or morbid drooping! The sympathy of the poet with the subjects of his poetry is particularly remarkable in Shakespeare and Chaucer; but what the first effects by a strong act of imagination and mental metamorphosis, the last does without any effort, merely by the inborn kindly joyousness of his nature. How well we seem to know Chaucer! How absolutely nothing do we know of Shakespeare!

I cannot in the least allow any necessity for Chaucer's poetry, especially the *Canterbury Tales*, being considered obsolete. Let a few plain rules be given for sounding the final *è* of syllables, and for expressing the termination of such words as *oceän*, and *nation*, etc., as dissyllables, or let the syllables to be sounded in such cases be marked by a competent metrist. This simple expedient would, with a very few trifling exceptions, where the errors are inveterate, enable any reader to feel the perfect smoothness and harmony of Chaucer's verse. As to understanding his language, if you read twenty pages with a good glossary, you surely can find no further difficulty. . . .

[1] As recorded by Henry Nelson Coleridge; first published in 1835, revised in 1836.

Matthew Arnold

from The Study of Poetry [1]

BUT in the fourteenth century there comes an Englishman nourished on this poetry, taught his trade by this poetry, getting words, rhyme, metre from this poetry; for even of that stanza which the Italians used, and which Chaucer derived immediately from the Italians, the basis and suggestion was probably given in France. Chaucer (I have already named him) fascinated his contemporaries, but so too did Christian of Troyes and Wolfram of Eschenbach. Chaucer's power of fascination, however, is enduring; his poetical importance does not need the assistance of the historic estimate; it is real. He is a genuine source of joy and strength, which is flowing still for us and will flow always. He will be read, as time goes on, far more generally than he is read now. His language is a cause of difficulty for us; but so also, and I think in quite as great a degree, is the language of Burns. In Chaucer's case, as in that of Burns, it is a difficulty to be unhesitatingly accepted and overcome.

If we ask ourselves wherein consists the immense superiority of Chaucer's poetry over the romance-poetry—why it is that in passing from this to Chaucer we suddenly feel ourselves to be in another world, we shall find that his superiority is both in the substance of his poetry and in the style of his poetry. His superiority in substance is given by his large, free, simple, clear yet kindly view of human life,—so unlike the total want, in the romance-poets, of all intelligent command of it. Chaucer has not their helplessness; he has gained the power to survey the world from a central, a truly human point of view. We have only to call

to mind the Prologue to *The Canterbury Tales*. The right comment upon it is Dryden's: "It is sufficient to say, according to the proverb, that *here is God's plenty*." And again: "He is a perpetual fountain of good sense." It is by a large, free, sound representation of things, that poetry, this high criticism of life, has truth of substance; and Chaucer's poetry has truth of substance.

Of his style and manner, if we think first of the romance-poetry and then of Chaucer's divine liquidness of diction, his divine fluidity of movement, it is difficult to speak temperately. They are irresistible, and justify all the rapture with which his successors speak of his "gold dew-drops of speech." [2] Johnson misses the point entirely when he finds fault with Dryden for ascribing to Chaucer the first refinement of our numbers, and says that Gower also can show smooth numbers and easy rhymes. The refinement of our numbers means something far more than this. A nation may have versifiers with smooth numbers and easy rhymes, and yet may have no real poetry at all. Chaucer is the father of our splendid English poetry; he is our "well of English undefiled," because by the lovely charm of his diction, the lovely charm of his movement, he makes an epoch and founds a tradition. In Spenser, Shakespeare, Milton, Keats, we can follow the tradition of the liquid diction, the fluid movement, of Chaucer; at one time it is his liquid diction of which in these poets we feel the virtue, and at another time it is his fluid movement. And the virtue is irresistible.

Bounded as is my space, I must yet find

---

[1] First published in 1880, as general introduction to *The English Poets*.

[2] For the context in which this tribute to Chaucer appears, see Muscatine's quotation from Lydgate's *The Life of Our Lady*, page 62, below.

room for an example of Chaucer's virtue, as I have given examples to show the virtue of the great classics. I feel disposed to say that a single line is enough to show the charm of Chaucer's verse; that merely one line like this—

"O martyr souded in virginitee!"   B 1769

has a virtue of manner and movement such as we shall not find in all the verse of romance-poetry;—but this is saying nothing. The virtue is such as we shall not find, perhaps, in all English poetry, outside the poets whom I have named as the special inheritors of Chaucer's tradition. A single line, however, is too little if we have not the strain of Chaucer's verse well in our memory; let us take a stanza. It is from *The Prioress's Tale*, the story of the Christian child murdered in a Jewry—

> "My throte is cut unto my nekke-bone
> Saidè this child, and as by way of kinde
> I should have deyd, yea, longè time agone;
> But Jesu Christ, as ye in bookès finde,
> Will that his glory last and be in minde,
> And for the worship of his mother dere
> Yet may I sing O Alma loud and
>   clere."   B 1845

Wordsworth has modernized this Tale, and to feel how delicate and evanescent is the charm of verse, we have only to read Wordsworth's first three lines of this stanza after Chaucer's—

> "My throat is cut unto the bone, I trow,
> Said this young child, and by the law of kind
> I should have died, yea, many hours ago."

The charm is departed. It is often said that the power of liquidness and fluidity in Chaucer's verse was dependent upon a free, a licentious dealing with language, such as is now impossible; upon a liberty, such as Burns too enjoyed, of making words like *neck, bird*, into a dissyllable by adding to them, and words like *cause, rhyme*, into a dissyllable by sounding the *e* mute. It is true that Chaucer's fluidity is conjoined with this liberty, and is admirably served by it; but we ought not to say that it was

dependent upon it. It was dependent upon his talent. Other poets with a like liberty do not attain to the fluidity of Chaucer; Burns himself does not attain to it. Poets, again, who have a talent akin to Chaucer's, such as Shakespeare or Keats, have known how to attain to his fluidity without the like liberty.

And yet Chaucer is not one of the great classics. His poetry transcends and effaces, easily and without effort, all the romance-poetry of Catholic Christendom; it transcends and effaces all the English poetry contemporary with it; it transcends and effaces all the English poetry subsequent to it down to the age of Elizabeth. Of such avail is poetic truth of substance, in its natural and necessary union with poetic truth of style. And yet, I say, Chaucer is not one of the great classics. He has not their accent. What is wanting to him is suggested by the mere mention of the name of the first great classic of Christendom, the immortal poet who died eighty years before Chaucer—Dante. The accent of such verse as

"In la sua volontade è nostra pace . . ."

is altogether beyond Chaucer's reach; we praise him, but we feel that this accent is out of the question for him. It may be said that it was necessarily out of the reach of any poet in the England of that stage of growth. Possibly; but we are to adopt a real, not a historic, estimate of poetry. However we may account for its absence, something is wanting, then, to the poetry of Chaucer, which poetry must have before it can be placed in the glorious class of the best. And there is no doubt what that something is. It is the σπουδαιότης, the high and excellent seriousness, which Aristotle assigns as one of the grand virtues of poetry. The substance of Chaucer's poetry, his view of things and his criticism of life, has largeness, freedom, shrewdness, benignity; but it has not this high seriousness. Homer's criticism of life has it, Dante's has it, Shakespeare's has it. It is this chiefly which gives to our spirits what they can rest upon; and with the increasing demands of our modern ages upon poetry, this virtue of giving us what we can rest upon will be more and more highly esteemed. A voice from the slums of Paris, fifty or sixty years after Chaucer, the voice of poor Villon out of his life of riot and crime, has at its happy moments (as, for instance, in the last stanza of *La Belle Heaulmière* [3]) more of this important poetic virtue of seriousness than all the productions of Chaucer. But its apparition in Villon, and in men like Villon, is fitful; the greatness of the great poets, the power of their criticism of life, is that their virtue is sustained.

To our praise, therefore, of Chaucer as a poet there must be this limitation; he lacks the high seriousness of the great classics, and therewith an important part of their virtue. Still, the main fact for us to bear in mind about Chaucer is his sterling value according to that real estimate which we firmly adopt for all poets. He has poetic truth of substance, though he has not high poetic seriousness, and corresponding to his truth of substance he has an exquisite virtue of style and manner. With him is born our real poetry.

---

[3] The name *Heaulmière* is said to be derived from a headdress (helm) worn as a mark by courtesans. In Villon's ballad, a poor old creature of this class laments her days of youth and beauty. The last stanza of the ballad runs thus—

"Ainsi le bon temps regretons
Entre nous, pauvres vieilles sottes,
Assises bas, à croppetons,
Tout en ung tas comme pelottes;
A petit feu de chenevottes
Tost allumées, tost estainctes.
Et jadis fusmes si mignottes!
Ainsi en prend à maintz et maintes."

"Thus amongst ourselves we regret the good time, poor silly old things, low-seated on our heels, all in a heap like so many balls; by a little fire of hemp-stalks, soon lighted, soon spent. And once we were such darlings! So fares it with many and many a one."

Arthur W. Hoffman

Chaucer's Prologue to Pilgrimage:
The Two Voices

CRITICISM of the portraits in Chaucer's General Prologue to *The Canterbury Tales* has taken various directions: some critics have praised the portraits especially for their realism, sharp individuality, adroit psychology, and vividness of felt life; others, working in the genetic directions, have pointed out actual historical persons who might have sat for the portraits; others, appealing to the light of the medieval sciences, have shown the portraits to be filled, though not burdened, with the lore of Chaucer's day, and to have sometimes typical identities like case histories. Miss Bowden,[1] in her recent study of the Prologue, assembles the fruits of many earlier studies and gives the text an impressive resonance by sketching historical and social norms and ideals, the facts and the standards of craft, trade, and profession, so that the form of the portraits can be tested in the light of possible conformities, mean or noble, to things as they were or to things as they ought to have been.

It is not unlikely that the critics who have explored in these various directions would be found in agreement on one commonplace, a metaphor which some of them indeed have used, the designation of the portraits in the General Prologue as figures in a tapestry. It is less likely that all of the critics would agree as to the implications of this metaphor, but it seems to me that the commonplace deserves to be explored and some of its implications tested. The commonplace implies that the portraits

[1] Muriel Bowden, *A Commentary on the General Prologue to the Canterbury Tales* (New York, 1948).

which appear in the General Prologue have a designed togetherness, that the portraits exist as parts of a unity.

Such a unity, it may be argued, is partly a function of the exterior framework of a pilgrimage to Canterbury; all the portraits are portraits of pilgrims:

> At nyght was come into that hostelrye
> Wel nyne and twenty in a compaignye,
> Of sondry folk, by aventure yfalle
> In felaweshipe, and pilgrimes were they
> alle,   A 26

But the unity of the Prologue may be also partly a matter of internal relationships among the portraits, relationships which are many and various among "sondry folk." One cannot hope to survey all of these, but the modest objective of studying some of the aesthetically important internal relationships is feasible.

If one begins with the unity that is exterior to the portraits, the unity that contains them, one faces directly the question of the nature of pilgrimage as it is defined in this dramatic poem. What sort of framework does the Prologue in fact define? Part of the answer is in the opening lines, and it is not a simple answer because the definition there ranges from the upthrust and burgeoning of life as a seasonal and universal event to a particular outpouring of people, pilgrims, gathered briefly at the Tabard Inn in Southwark, drifting, impelled, bound, called to the shrine of Thomas à Becket at Canterbury. The pilgrimage is set down in the calendar of seasons as well as in the calendar of piety; nature impels and supernature draws. "Go,

Reprinted by permission of author and editor from *ELH*, XXI (1954), 1-16.

go, go," says the bird; "Come," says the saint.

In the opening lines of the Prologue springtime is characterized in terms of procreation, and a pilgrimage of people to Canterbury is just one of the many manifestations of the life thereby produced. The phallicism of the opening lines presents the impregnating of a female March by a male April, and a marriage of water and earth. The marriage is repeated and varied immediately as a fructifying of "holt and heeth" by Zephirus, a marriage of air and earth. This mode of symbolism and these symbols as parts of a rite of spring have a long background of tradition; as Professor Cook [2] once pointed out, there are eminent passages of this sort in Aeschylus and Euripides, in Lucretius, in Virgil's *Georgics*, in Columella, and in the *Pervigilium Veneris*, and Professor Robinson cites Guido delle Colonne, Boccaccio, Petrarch, and Boethius. Zephirus is the only overt mythological figure in Chaucer's passage, but, in view of the instigative role generally assigned to Aphrodite in the rite of spring, she is perhaps to be recognized here, as Professor Cook suggested, in the name of April, which was her month both by traditional association and by one of the two ancient etymologies.[3] Out of this context of the quickening of the earth presented naturally and symbolically in the broadest terms, the Prologue comes to pilgrimage and treats pilgrimage first as an event in the calendar of nature, one aspect of the general springtime surge of human energy and longing. There are the attendant suggestions of the renewal of human mobility after the rigor and confinement of winter, the revival of wayfaring now that the ways are open. The horizon extends to distant shrines and foreign lands, and the attraction of the strange and faraway is included before the vision

[2] Albert S. Cook, "Chaucerian Papers—I: I. Prologue 1–11," *Transactions of the Connecticut Academy of Arts and Sciences,* XXIII (New Haven, 1919), 5–21.
[3] Cook, 5–10.

narrows and focuses upon its English specifications and the pilgrimage to the shrine at Canterbury with the vows and gratitude that send pilgrims there. One way of regarding the structure of this opening passage would emphasize the magnificent progression from the broadest inclusive generality to the firmest English specification, from the whole western tradition of the celebration of spring (including, as Cook pointed out, such a non-English or very doubtfully English detail as "the droghte of March") to a local event of English society and English Christendom, from natural forces in their most general operation to a very specific and Christian manifestation of those forces. And yet one may regard the structure in another way, too; if, in the calendar of nature, the passage moves from general to particular, does it not, in the calendar of piety, move from nature to something that includes and oversees nature? Does not the passage move from an activity naturally generated and impelled to a governed activity, from force to *telos?* Does not the passage move from Aphrodite and *amor* in their secular operation to the sacred embrace of "the hooly blisful martir" and of *amor dei?*

The transition from nature to supernature is emphasized by the contrast between the healthful physical vigor of the opening lines and the reference to sickness that appears in line 18. On the one hand, it is physical vitality which conditions the pilgrimage; on the other hand, sickness occasions pilgrimage. It is, in fact, rather startling to come upon the word "seeke" at the end of this opening passage, because it is like a breath of winter across the landscape of spring. "Whan that they were seeke" may, of course, refer literally to illnesses of the winter just past, but, in any event, illness belongs symbolically to the inclement season. There is also, however, a strong parallelism between the beginning and end of this passage, a parallelism that has to do with restorative power. The physical vitality of the opening is presented as restorative of the dry earth; the power of the saint is presented as restorative of the sick. The seasonal restoration of nature parallels a supernatural kind of restoration that knows no season; the supernatural kind of restoration involves a wielding and directing of the forces of nature. The Prologue begins, then, by presenting a double view of the Canterbury pilgrimage: the pilgrimage is one tiny manifestation of a huge tide of life, but then, too, the tide of life ebbs and flows in response to the power which the pilgrimage acknowledges, the power symbolized by "the hooly blisful martir."

After line 18 the process of particularizing is continued, moving from "that seson" just defined to a day and to a place and to a person in Southwark at the Tabard, and thence to the portraits of the pilgrims. The double view of pilgrimage is enhanced and extended by the portraits where it appears, in one aspect, as a range of motivation. This range of motivation is from the sacred to the secular and on to the profane—"profane" in the sense of motivations actually subversive of the sacred. All the pilgrims are, in fact, granted an ostensible sacred motive; all of them are seeking the shrine. The distances that we are made aware of are both *within* some of the portraits, where a gulf yawns between ostensible and actual motivation, and *between* the portraits, where the motivation of the Knight and the Parson is near one end of the spectrum, and the motivation of the Summoner and the Pardoner near the other end. There is such an impure but blameless mixture as the motivation of the Prioress; there is the secular pilgrimage of the Wife of Bath, impelled so powerfully and frankly by Saint Venus rather than drawn by Saint Thomas, and goaded by a Martian desire to acquire and dominate another husband; in the case of the Prioress, an inescapable doubt as to the quality of *amor* hesitates between the sacred and secular, and in the case of the thoroughly secular Wife of Bath, doubt hesitates between the secular and the profane while the portrait shows the ostensible motive that belongs to all the pilgrims shaken without ever being subverted, contradicted perhaps, brazenly opposed, but still acknowledged and offered, not, at any rate, hypocritically betrayed. In the area of motivation, the portraits seem to propose, ultimately, a fundamental, inescapable ambiguity as part of the human condition; prayer for the purification of motive is valid for all the pilgrims. And the pilgrims who move, pushed by impulse and drawn by vows, none merely impelled and none perfectly committed, reflect, in their human ambiguity, the broad problem of origins and ends, the stubbornness of matter and the power of spirit, together with ideas of cosmic resolution and harmony in which source and end are reconciled and seem to be the same, the purposes of nature and supernature found to be at one, the two restorative powers akin, the kinds of love not discontinuous, Saint Venus and Saint Thomas different and at odds yet not at war, within the divine purpose which contains both.

The portraits of the Knight and the Squire have a particular interest. The relationships between these two portraits are governed by and arise out of the natural relationship of father and son. Consanguinity provides the base for a dramatic relationship, and at the same time is the groundwork for a modestly generalized metaphor of age and youth. Each portrait is enhanced and defined by the presence of the other: the long roll of the Knight's campaigns, and the Squire's little opportunity ("so litel space"), a few raids enumerated in one line; a series of past tenses, a history, for the Knight, and for the Squire a present breaking forth in active participles; the Knight not "gay," wearing fustian soiled by his coat of mail, "bismotered," the Squire bright and fresh and colorful; the Knight meek and quiet,—or so the portrait leaves him—beside the Squire, who sings and whistles all the day. The Knight's love is an achieved devotion, a matter of pledges fulfilled and of values, if not completely realized, yet woven into the fabric of experience (ideals—"trouthe," "honour," "fredom," "curteisie"). The Squire is a lover, a warm and eager lover, paying court to his lady and sleeping no more than the nightingale. In the one, the acquired, tutored, disciplined, elevated, enlarged love, the piety; and in the other, the love channelled into an elaborate social ritual, a parody piety, but still emphatically fresh and full of natural impulse. One cannot miss the creation of the Squire in conventional images of nature, the meadow, the flowers, the freshness like May, the lover like the nightingale,—comparisons that are a kind of re-emergence of the opening lines of the Prologue, the springtime surge of youthful, natural energy that animates the beginning. "Go, go, go," the bird's voice, is a major impulse in the portrait of the Squire and in the Squire's pilgrimage; the Knight's pilgrimage is more nearly a response to the voice of the saint. Yet the Squire is within the belt of rule, and learning the calendar of piety. The concluding couplet of the portrait

> Curteis he was, lowely and servysable,
> And carf biforn his fader at the table.   A 100

has the effect of bending all the youth, energy, color, audibleness, and high spirit of the Squire to the service of his father, the Knight, and to attendance on his pilgrimage, with perhaps a suggestion of the present submitting to the serious and respected values served and communicated by the past, the natural and the imposed submitting of the son to his natural father, and beyond him to the supernatural goal, the shrine to which the father directs his pilgrimage.

The portraits of the Knight and the Squire represent one of the ways in which portraiture takes into account and develops the double definition of pilgrimage which is established at the beginning. The double definition of pilgrimage is involved in a different way in the portrait of the Prioress; there it appears as a delicately poised am-

biguity. Two definitions appear as two faces of one coin. Subsequently, when the portrait of the Prioress is seen together with the portraits of the Monk and the Friar, a sequence is realized, running from ambiguity to emphatic discrepancy, and the satire that circles the impenetrable duality of sacred and secular impulse in the case of the Prioress, knifes in as these impulses are drawn apart in the case of the Monk and strikes vigorously in the still wider breach that appears in the case of the Friar. What is illustrated within the portraits is amplified by a designed sequence.

The delicate balance in the picture of the Prioress has been generally recognized and has perhaps been only the more clearly exhibited by occasional seesawing in the critical interpretation of the portrait in which the satiric elements are sometimes represented as heavy, sometimes as slight, sometimes sinking the board, and sometimes riding light and high. There is, perhaps, no better illustration of the delicacy of the balance than the fact that the Prioress's very presence on a pilgrimage, as several commentators have pointed out, may be regarded as the first satiric touch. The very act of piety is not free from the implication of imperfection; the Prioress is obligated to a cloistered piety that serves and worships God without going on a journey to seek a shrine, and prioresses were specifically and repeatedly enjoined from going on pilgrimages. Prioresses did, nevertheless, go as pilgrims, so that Chaucer's Prioress is not departing from the norm of behavior of persons in her office so much as she is departing from the sanctioned ideal of behavior.[4] In the case of the Prioress, the blemish is sufficiently technical to have only faint satiric coloring; it is not the notable kind of blemish recognized in all times and all places. Nevertheless, it is precisely this kind of hint of a spot that places the

---

[4] The relevance of the ideal sanctioned character of an office to the portrait of a person will appear again strikingly in the case of the Summoner and the Pardoner.

Prioress at one end of a sequence in which the more obviously blemished Monk and Friar appear. If we pose a double question —What kind of woman is the Prioress, and what kind of prioress is the woman?—the portrait responds more immediately to the first part of the question, and leaves the answer to the second part largely in the area of implication. The portrait occupies forty-five lines, and more than three-fourths of the lines have to do with such matters as the Prioress's blue eyes, her red mouth, the shape of her nose and width of her forehead, her ornaments and dress, her table manners, her particular brand of French, her pets and what she fed them, and her tenderness about mice. It is, of course, one of the skilful arts of these portraits to work with surfaces and make the surfaces convey and reveal what lies beneath, but it should be observed that in the case of the Parson—or even in the case of the Knight—a character is arrived at almost entirely without physical and superficial detail. One need not take the emphatic surface in the portrait of the Prioress as necessarily pejorative in its implication; it need not follow that the Prioress is a shallow and superficial person, and, in consequence, sharply satirized. But the portrait does seem, by means of its emphasis on surfaces, to define the Prioress as woman, and strongly enough so that tension between the person and her office, between the given human nature and the assumed sacred obligation is put vividly before us, and rather as the observation of a fact than as the instigation of a judgment. In the cases of the Monk and the Friar, the tension is so exacerbated that judgment is, in the case of the Monk, incited, and in the case of the Friar, both incited and inflamed to severity.

In the portrait of the Prioress the double view of pilgrimage appears both in an ambiguity of surfaces, and in an implied inner range of motivation. In the surfaces there is a sustained hovering effect: the name, Eglentyne, is romance, and "simple and coy" is a romance formula, but she *is* a nun,

by whatever name, and "simple" and "coy," aside from their romance connotations, have meanings ("simple" and "modest") appropriate enough to a nun; there are the coral beads and the green gauds, but they *are* a rosary; there are the fluted wimple and the exposed forehead, but the costume *is* a nun's habit; there is the golden brooch shining brightly, but it *is* a religious emblem. Which shall be taken as principal, which as modifying and subordinate? Are the departures or the conformities more significant of her nature? Are her Stratford French and her imitation of court manners more important than the fact that she sings well and properly the divine service? Do we detect vanity in her singing well, or do we rely on what she sings and accept her worship as well performed—to the glory of God? The ambiguity of these surface indications leads into the implied range of motivation; this implied range has been generally recognized in the motto—"*Amor vincit omnia*"—on the Prioress's golden brooch, and the implications set up in the portrait as a whole seem to be clustered and tightly fastened in this ornament and symbol.

The motto itself has, in the course of history, gone its own double pilgrimage to the shrine of Saint Venus and to sacred shrines; the original province of the motto was profane, but it was drawn over to a sacred meaning and soon became complexly involved with and compactly significant of both. Professor Lowes comments on the motto as it pertains to the Prioress:

Now is it earthly love that conquers all, now heavenly; the phrase plays back and forth between the two. And it is precisely that happy ambiguity of the convention—itself the result of an earlier transfer—that makes Chaucer's use of it here . . . a master stroke. *Which of the two loves does "amor" mean to the Prioress?* I do not know; but I think she thought she meant love celestial.[5]

---

[5] John Livingston Lowes, *Convention and Revolt in Poetry* (Boston, 1919), p. 66.

Professor Lowes, presumably, does not really expect to see the matter concluded one way or the other and finds this very inconclusiveness, hovering between two answers, one of the excellences of the portrait. There is, however, a certain amount of illumination to be gained, though not an answer to the question as formulated by Professor Lowes, by asking the question another way and considering an answer in terms that lie outside of the Prioress's motivation. Put the question in this form: Which of the two loves does the *portrait* in the context of the Prologue mean by *amor?* The answer to this question, of course, is *both.* On the one hand, profane love or the love of earthly things does overcome all; the little vanities and pretensions, the love of color and decoration and dress, the affection squandered in little extravagances toward pets, the pity and tender emotion wasted upon a trapped mouse—the multiplicity of secular, impulsive loves threatens to and could ultimately stifle the dedication to the celestial love. This answer is, in fact, a version of the Prioress's character and motivation sometimes offered. It actually implies one half of the view of pilgrimage—the natural powers that move people and that may usurp the whole character. But the other answer—celestial love conquers all things—also applies to the portrait, though it is not very easily arrived at in terms of the Prioress's motivation. Here we are dealing with the ostensible meaning of the motto, the ideal meaning of the motto as worn by a prioress—what it ought to mean in terms of her office. And, no matter what the impurity of the Prioress's motives, no matter what she means or thinks she means by the motto, the motto does, in the calendar of piety, mean that God's love is powerful over all things, powerful in this case over the vanity that may be involved in the wearing of the brooch, powerful over all the shallowness and limitation and reduction and misdirection of love that the Prioress may be guilty of, powerful over all her departures from or misunderstandings of dis-

cipline and obligation and vow, powerful over all inadequacy, able to overcome the faults of God's human instruments and make this woman's divine office valid. The motto, and the portrait of which it is the conclusion, appreciate both the secular impulses and the sacred redemptive will, but there is no doubt which love it is that is crowned with ultimate power.

Chaucer has found ways, as in the case of the Prioress, of making an ideal or standard emerge within a portrait. The standard may be ambiguously stated or heavily involved in irony, but it is almost always present, and nowhere with greater effectiveness than in the most sharply satiric portraits. This, I take it, is the effect of the formula of worthiness which is applied to so many of the pilgrims. A character is declared to be "worthy" or "the best that ever was" of his craft or profession or office, and frequently under circumstances that make the statement jarring and the discrepancy obvious. There is a definite shock, for example, when Friar Huberd is declared to be a "worthy lymytour," or the Pardoner "a noble ecclesiaste." Even when the satiric thrust has two directions, striking both at the individual and at the group to which he belongs, the implication has nevertheless been lodged in the portrait that there could be, for example, a worthy friar, or a pardoner who was indeed a noble ecclesiastic. The reader is, as it were, tripped in the act of judging and reminded that if he condemns these figures, if they appear culpable, there must be some sort of standard by which they are so judged, by which they appear so.

Chaucer has also adopted the method of including ideal or nearly ideal portraits among the pilgrims. There are, for example, the Knight and the Plowman, figures at either end of the secular range, and among the clerical figures there is the Parson. A host of relative judgments, of course, are set up by devices of sequence and obvious pairing and contrasting of portraits. It is the ideal portraits, however, that somehow preside over all these judgments and comparisons, and it is to them that the relative distinctions are presented for a kind of penultimate judgment. Prioress, Monk, and Friar, and all the other clerical figures are reckoned with the Parson who is, in fact, made to speak in an accent of judgment upon the clerical figures who go astray—". . . if gold ruste, what shal iren do?" (We may remember the Prioress's shining gold brooch, the Monk's gold pin, and, among the secular figures, the Physician who so doubly regarded gold as a sovereign remedy.)

Chaucer has used an interesting device for undergirding the ideal portrait of the Parson. He employs consanguinity with metaphorical effect. After the assertions which declare that the Parson "first . . . wroghte, and afterward . . . taughte," the actualizing of Christian ideals is supported by the representation of the Parson as brother to the Plowman. It is the Parson's Christian obligation to treat men as brothers, and the portrait abundantly affirms that he does so. Making him actually the brother of the Plowman brilliantly insists that what supernature calls for is performed by the Parson and, more than that, comes by nature to him.[6] The achieved harmony both comes from above and rises out of the ground; sacred and secular are linked, the shepherd of souls and the tiller of the soil. This is a vantage point from which the conflicts of secular and sacred, of nature and supernature, are seen in a revealing light, a point at which one sees reflected in the clear mirror of ideal characters and an actual-ideal relationship the fundamental double view of pilgrimage established in the beginning.

The double definition of pilgrimage is differently but nonetheless revealingly illuminated by the portraits of another fraternizing pair, the Summoner and Pardoner,

who conclude the sequence of pilgrims. The illumination here is not clarified by way of ideal characters but somehow refracted and intensified by the dark surfaces upon which it falls. The darkness is most visible in connection with the theme of love, which appears here in a sinister and terrible distortion. The hot and lecherous Summoner, the type of sexual unrestraint, is represented as harmonizing in song with the impotent Pardoner, the eunuch; the deep rumbling voice and the thin effeminate voice are singing, "Com hider, love, to me!" The song, in this context, becomes both a promiscuous and perverted invitation and an unconscious symbolic acknowledgment of the absence of and the need for love, love that comes neither to the grasping physical endeavor of the Summoner nor to the physical incapacity of the Pardoner—nor to their perverted spirits. Love has been treated in the Prologue from the beginning as dual in character, a matter both of the body and the spirit, the *amor* symbolized by Venus, sung by the Squire, equivocally illustrated by the Prioress, lustily celebrated by the Wife of Bath; and the *amor dei*, the love shadowily there beyond all the secular forms of love, a hovering presence among the pilgrims and sometimes close, as to the Knight and the Parson and the Plowman, and symbolized in the saint's shrine which is the goal of all of them. On this view, the song of the Summoner and the Pardoner is a superb dramatic irony acknowledging the full extent of their need and loss, the love of God which they ought to strive for, the love which they desperately need.

The office which each of these men is supposed to fulfill should be taken into account. The Summoner is, ostensibly, an instrument through whom divine justice, in a practical way, operates in the world. There are, in the portrait, a few touches that may be reminders of the ultimate source of his authority and function: his "*Questio quid iuris*," though it is represented satirically as the sum and substance of his knowledge, and posed as a question, *is* legitimately the

---

[6] There is, of course, plenty of actual basis for representing a parson as a son of the soil; the connection is not merely an artistic and symbolic device.

substance of his knowledge—his province is law, especially the divine law; "*Significavit*" is the opening word of a legal writ, a dreaded worldly pronouncement of divine judgment, excommunication; he is physically a fearful figure from whom children run (not the divine love which suffers them to come), and some of the physical details may be reminders of noble and awesome aspects of divine justice—his "fyr-reed cherubynnes face" and the voice described in a significant analogy as like a trumpet, "Was nevere trompe of half so greet a soun." The Pardoner, on the other hand, is the ostensible instrument of divine mercy and love. Many of the pardoners, as Miss Bowden points out, went so far as to pretend to absolve both *a poena* and *a culpa*, thereby usurping, in the pretended absolution *a culpa*, a function which theological doctrine reserved to God and His grace. In any case, their legitimate functions were an appeal for charity and an extension of God's mercy and love. The Pardoner, it should be observed, is, compared to the Summoner, an attractive figure. We may be reminded of the superior affinity of the Pardoner's office by the veil which he has sewed upon his cap, the copy of St. Veronica's veil which is supposed to have received the imprint of Christ's face.[7]

The justice and love[8] of which the Sum-

[7] Later, in telling his story, the Pardoner acknowledges that his pardons are inferior versions of the supreme pardon which is Christ's. See *The Pardoner's Tale*, 915–918.

[8] This statement of the symbolic values behind the Summoner and the Pardoner is not a disagreement with, but merely an addition to, the point made by Kellogg and Haselmayer (Alfred L. Kellogg and Louis A. Haselmayer, "Chaucer's Satire of the Pardoner," *PMLA*, LXVI [March, 1951], 215–277) when they assert: "In this paradox, this ironic portrait of justice and crime singing in close harmony, we reach the center of Chaucer's satire." (p. 275) There is, indeed, the strongest satiric impact in this affiliation of the man who should apprehend the wrongdoer with the criminal. In addition, however, if we are to see beyond the Summoner's disabilities to his representation of justice, we see in parallel vision beyond the Pardoner's disabilities a representation of love.

moner and Pardoner are emissaries are properly complementary and harmoniously, though paradoxically and mysteriously, related, so that the advances that are being made both of persons and of values are, in a very serious sense, proper to this pair. The radical physical distinctness of Summoner and Pardoner is at this level the definition of two aspects of supernature; there is the same employment of physical metaphor here that there is in the portraits of the Parson and the Plowman, but with the difference that light comes out of darkness, and out of the gravest corruption of nature the supernatural relationship emerges clarified in symbol. The Summoner cannot finally pervert, and the Pardoner's impotence cannot finally prevent; the divine justice and love are powerful even over these debased instruments—*Amor vincit omnia*. Beyond their knowing, beyond their power or impotence, impotently both Pardoner and Summoner appeal for the natural love—melody of bird-song and meadows of flowers—and both pray for the celestial love, the ultimate pardon which in their desperate and imprisoned darkness is their only hope: "Com hider, love, to me!"

The exterior unity achieved by the realistic device and broadly symbolic framework of pilgrimage is made stronger and tighter in the portraits, partly by local sequences and pairings, but most impressively by the illustration, the variation and enrichment by way of human instances, of a theme of love, earthly and celestial, and a general complex intermingling of the consideration of nature with the consideration of supernature. The note of love is sounded in different keys all through the portraits:

The Knight

. . . he loved chivalrie,
Trouthe and honour, fredom and
    curteisie   A 46

The Squire

A lovyere and a lusty bacheler . . .   80
So hoote he lovede that by nyghtertale

He sleep namoore than dooth a
nyghtyngale.

The Prioress
    ... *Amor vincit omnia.*   162

The Monk
A Monk ... that lovede venerie, ...   166
He hadde of gold ywroght a ful curious pyn;
A love-knotte in the gretter ende ther was.   197
A fat swan loved he best of any roost.   206

The Friar
In love-dayes ther koude he muchel
    help ...   258
Somewhat he lipsed, for his
    wantownesse, ...   264

The Clerk
For hym was levere have at his beddes heed
Twenty bookes, clad in blak or reed,
Of Aristotle and his philosophie,
Than robes riche, or fithele, or gay sautrie.   296

The Frankelyn
Wel loved he by the morwe a sop in wyn;
To lyven in delit was evere his wone,
For he was Epicurus owene sone ...   336

The Physician
He kepte that he wan in pestilence.
For gold in phisik is a cordial,
Therefore he lovede gold in special.   444

The Wife of Bath
Of remedies of love she knew per chaunce,
For she koude of that art the olde daunce.   476

The Parson
But rather wolde he yeven, out of doute,
Unto his povre parisshens aboute
Of his offryng and eek of his substaunce.   489

    ... Cristes loore and his apostles twelve
He taughte, but first he folwed it
    hymselve.   528

The Plowman
With hym ther was a Plowman, was his
    brother, ...   529

Lyvynge in pees and parfit charitee.
God loved he best with al his hoole herte
At alle tymes, thogh him gamed or smerte,
And thanne his neighebor right as
    hymselve.   535

The Summoner and the Pardoner
    ... "Com hider, love, to me!"   672

The theme of restorative power attends
upon the theme of love. It is, of course, announced at the beginning and defined in
terms both of nature and supernature. Both
the Physician, concerned with natural healing, and the Pardoner, the agent of a supernatural healing, appear under the rubric of
"Physician, heal thyself." The worldly
Physician is disaffected from God; the Pardoner is naturally impotent. Serious inadequacy in either realm appears as counterpart of inadequacy in the other. It is the
Parson who both visits the sick and tends
properly to the cure of souls; he works
harmoniously in both realms, and both
realms are in harmony and fulfilled in him.

The pilgrims are represented as affected
by a variety of destructive and restorative
kinds of love. Their characters and movement can be fully described only as mix-
tures of the loves that drive and goad and
of the love that calls and summons. The
pilgrims have, while they stay and when
they move, their worldly host. They have,
too, their worldly Summoner and Pardoner
who, in the very worst way, move and are
moved with them. Nevertheless, the Summoner and Pardoner, who conclude the
roll of the company, despite and beyond
their appalling personal deficiency, may
suggest the summoning and pardoning, the
judgment and grace which in Christian
thought embrace and conclude man's pilgrimage and which therefore, with all the
corrosions of satire and irony, are also the
seriously appropriate conclusion to the
tapestry of Chaucer's pilgrims.

E. Talbot Donaldson

Chaucer the Pilgrim

VERISIMILITUDE in a work of fiction is not without its attendant dangers, the chief of which is that the responses it stimulates in the reader may be those appropriate not so much to an imaginative production as to an historical one or to a piece of reporting. History and reporting are, of course, honorable in themselves, but if we react to a poet as though he were an historian or a reporter, we do him somewhat less than justice. I am under the impression that many readers, too much influenced by Chaucer's brilliant verisimilitude, tend to regard his famous pilgrimage to Canterbury as significant not because it is a great fiction, but because it seems to be a remarkable record of a fourteenth-century pilgrimage. A remarkable record it may be, but if we treat it too narrowly as such there are going to be certain casualties among the elements that make up the fiction. Perhaps first among these elements is the fictional reporter, Chaucer the pilgrim, and the role he plays in the Prologue to the *Canterbury Tales* and in the links between them. I think it time that he was rescued from the comparatively dull record of history and put back into his poem. He is not really Chaucer the poet—nor, for that matter, is either the poet, or the poem's protagonist, that Geoffrey Chaucer frequently mentioned in contemporary historical records as a distinguished civil servant, but never as a poet. The fact that these are three separate entities does not, naturally, exclude the probability—or rather the certainty—that they bore a close resemblance to one another, and that, indeed, they frequently got together in the same body. But

that does not excuse us from keeping them distinct from one another, difficult as their close resemblance makes our task.

The natural tendency to confuse one thing with its like is perhaps best represented by a school of Chaucerian criticism, now outmoded, that pictured a single Chaucer under the guise of a wide-eyed, jolly, roly-poly little man who, on fine Spring mornings, used to get up early, while the dew was still on the grass, and go look at daisies. A charming portrait, this, so charming, indeed, that it was sometimes able to maintain itself to the exclusion of any Chaucerian other side. It has every reason to be charming, since it was lifted almost *in toto* from the version Chaucer gives of himself in the Prologue to the *Legend of Good Women,* though I imagine it owes some of its popularity to a rough analogy with Wordsworth— a sort of *Legend of Good Poets.* It was this version of Chaucer that Kittredge, in a page of great importance to Chaucer criticism, demolished with his assertion that "a naïf Collector of Customs would be a paradoxical monster." He might well have added that a naïve creator of old January would be even more monstrous.

Kittredge's pronouncement cleared the air, and most of us now accept the proposition that Chaucer was sophisticated as readily as we do the proposition that the whale is a mammal. But unhappily, now that we've got rid of the naïve fiction, it is easy to fall into the opposite sort of mistake. This is to envision, in the *Canterbury Tales,* a highly urbane, literal-historical Chaucer setting out from Southwark on a specific day of a specific year (we even argue somewhat

Reprinted by permission from *PMLA,* LXIX (1954), 928–936.

acrimoniously about dates and routes), in company with a group of persons who existed in real life and whom Chaucer, his reporter's eye peeled for every idiosyncrasy, determined to get down on paper—down, that is, to the last wart—so that books might be written identifying them. Whenever this accurate reporter says something especially fatuous—which is not infrequently—it is either ascribed to an opinion peculiar to the Middle Ages (sometimes very peculiar), or else Chaucer's tongue is said to be in his cheek.

Now a Chaucer with tongue-in-cheek is a vast improvement over a simple-minded Chaucer when one is trying to define the whole man, but it must lead to a loss of critical perception, and in particular to a confused notion of Chaucerian irony, to see in the Prologue a reporter who is acutely aware of the significance of what he sees but who sometimes, for ironic emphasis, interprets the evidence presented by his observation in a fashion directly contrary to what we expect. The proposition ought to be expressed in reverse: the reporter is, usually, acutely unaware of the significance of what he sees, no matter how sharply he sees it. He is, to be sure, permitted his lucid intervals, but in general he is the victim of the poet's pervasive—not merely sporadic—irony. And as such he is also the chief agent by which the poet achieves his wonderfully complex, ironic, comic, serious vision of a world which is but a devious and confused, infinitely various pilgrimage to a certain shrine. It is, as I hope to make clear, a good deal more than merely fitting that our guide on such a pilgrimage should be a man of such naïveté as the Chaucer who tells the tale of *Sir Thopas*. Let us accompany him a little distance.

It is often remarked that Chaucer really liked the Prioress very much, even though he satirized her gently—very gently. But this is an understatement: Chaucer the pilgrim may not be said merely to have liked the Prioress very much—he thought she was utterly charming. In the first twenty-odd lines of her portrait (A 118 ff.) he employs, among other superlatives, the adverb *ful* seven times. Middle English uses *ful* where we use *very*, and if one translates the beginning of the portrait into a kind of basic English (which is what, in a way, it really is), one gets something like this: "There was also a Nun, a Prioress, who was very sincere and modest in the way she smiled; her biggest oath was only 'By saint Loy'; and she was called Madame Eglantine. She sang the divine service very well, intoning it in her nose very prettily, and she spoke French very nicely and elegantly" —and so on, down to the last gasp of sentimental appreciation. Indeed, the Prioress may be said to have transformed the rhetoric into something not unlike that of a very bright kindergarten child's descriptive theme. In his reaction to the Prioress Chaucer the pilgrim resembles another—if less—simple-hearted enthusiast: the Host, whose summons to her to tell a tale must be one of the politest speeches in the language. Not "My lady prioresse, a tale now!" but, "as curteisly as it had been a mayde,"

My lady Prioresse, by youre leve,
So that I wiste I sholde yow nat greve,
I wolde demen that ye tellen sholde
A tale next, if so were that ye wolde.
Now wol ye vouche sauf, my lady
    deere?   B 1641

Where the Prioress reduced Chaucer to superlatives, she reduces the Host to subjunctives.

There is no need here to go deeply into the Prioress. Eileen Power's illustrations from contemporary episcopal records show with what extraordinary economy the portrait has been packed with abuses typical of fourteenth-century nuns. The abuses, to be sure, are mostly petty, but it is clear enough that the Prioress, while a perfect lady, is anything but a perfect nun; and attempts to whitewash her, of which there have been many, can only proceed from an innocence of heart equal to Chaucer the pilgrim's and undoubtedly directly influenced by it. For he, of course, is quite swept away by her irrelevant *sensibilité*, and as a result misses much of the point of what he sees. No doubt he feels that he has come a long way, socially speaking, since his encounter with the Black Knight in the forest, and he knows, or thinks he knows, a little more of what it's all about; in this case it seems to be mostly about good manners, kindness to animals, and female charm. Thus it has been argued that Chaucer's appreciation for the Prioress as a sort of heroine of courtly romance *manquée* actually reflects the sophistication of the living Chaucer, an urbane man who cared little whether amiable nuns were good nuns. But it seems a curious form of sophistication that permits itself to babble superlatives; and indeed, if this is sophistication, it is the kind generally seen in the least experienced people —one that reflects a wide-eyed wonder at the glamor of the great world. It is just what one might expect of a bourgeois exposed to the splendors of high society, whose values, such as they are, he eagerly accepts. And that is precisely what Chaucer the pilgrim is, and what he does.

If the Prioress's appeal to him is through elegant femininity, the Monk's is through imposing virility. Of this formidable and important prelate the pilgrim does not say, with Placebo,

> I woot wel that my lord kan moore than I:
> What that he seith, I holde it ferme and
>   stable,   E 1499

but he acts Placebo's part to perfection. He is as impressed with the Monk as the Monk is, and accepts him on his own terms and at face value, never sensing that those terms imply complete condemnation of Monk *qua* Monk. The Host is also impressed by the Monk's virility, but having no sense of Placebonian propriety (he is himself a most virile man) he makes indecent jokes about it. This, naturally, offends the pilgrim's sense of decorum: there is a note of deferential commiseration in his comment, "This

worthy Monk took al in pacience" (B 3155). Inevitably when the Monk establishes hunting as the highest activity of which religious man is capable, "I seyde his opinion was good" (A 183). As one of the pilgrim's spiritual heirs was later to say, Very like a whale; but not, of course, like a fish out of water.

Wholehearted approval for the values that important persons subscribe to is seen again in the portrait of the Friar. This amounts to a prolonged gratulation for the efficiency the deplorable Hubert shows in undermining the fabric of the Church by turning St. Francis' ideal inside out:

> Ful swetely herde he confessioun,
> And plesaunt was his absolucioun.   A 222

> For unto swich a worthy man as he
> Acorded nat, as by his facultee,
> To have with sike lazars aqueyntaunce.   245

It is sometimes said that Chaucer did not like the Friar. Whether Chaucer the man would have liked such a Friar is, for our present purposes, irrelevant. But if the pilgrim does not unequivocally express his liking for him, it is only because in his humility he does not feel that, with important people, his own likes and dislikes are material: such importance is its own reward, and can gain no lustre from Geoffrey, who, when the Friar is attacked by the Summoner, is ready to show him the same sympathy he shows the Monk (see D 1265–67).

Once he has finished describing the really important people on the pilgrimage the pilgrim's tone changes, for he can now concern himself with the bourgeoisie, members of his own class for whom he does not have to show such profound respect. Indeed, he can even afford to be a little patronizing at times, and to have his little joke at the expense of the too-busy lawyer. But such indirect assertions of his own superiority do not prevent him from giving substance to the old cynicism that the only motive recognized by the middle class is the profit motive, for his interest and admiration for the bourgeois pilgrims is centered mainly in their material prosperity and their ability to increase it. He starts, properly enough, with the out-and-out money-grubber, the Merchant, and after turning aside for that *lusus naturae*, the non-profit-motivated Clerk, proceeds to the Lawyer, who, despite the pilgrim's little joke, is the best and best-paid ever; the Franklin, twenty-one admiring lines on appetite, so expensively catered to; the Gildsmen, cheered up the social ladder, "For catel hadde they ynogh and rente" (A 373); and the Physician, again the best and richest. In this series the portrait of the Clerk is generally held to be an ideal one, containing no irony; but while it is ideal, it seems to reflect the pilgrim's sense of values in his joke about the Clerk's failure to make money: is not this still typical of the half-patronizing, half-admiring *un-understanding* that practical men of business display towards academics? But in any case the portrait is a fine companion-piece for those in which material prosperity is the main interest both of the characters described and of the describer.

Of course, this is not the sole interest of so gregarious—if shy—a person as Chaucer the pilgrim. Many of the characters have the additional advantage of being good companions, a faculty that receives a high valuation in the Prologue. To be good company might, indeed, atone for certain serious defects of character. Thus the Shipman, whose callous cruelty is duly noted, seems fairly well redeemed in the assertion, "And certeinly he was a good felawe" (A 395). At this point an uneasy sensation that even tongue-in-cheek irony will not compensate for the lengths to which Chaucer is going in his approbation of this sinister seafarer sometimes causes editors to note that *a good felawe* means "a rascal." But I can find no evidence that it ever meant a rascal. Of course, all tritely approbative expressions enter easily into ironic connotation, but the phrase *means* a good companion,

which is just what Chaucer means. And if, as he says of the Shipman, "Of nyce conscience took he no keep" (A 398), Chaucer the pilgrim was doing the same with respect to him.

Nothing that has been said has been meant to imply that the pilgrim was unable to recognize, and deplore, a rascal when he saw one. He could, provided the rascality was situated in a member of the lower classes and provided it was, in any case, somewhat wider than a barn door: Miller, Manciple, Reeve, Summoner, and Pardoner are all acknowledged to be rascals. But rascality generally has, after all, the laudable object of making money, which gives it a kind of validity, if not dignity. These portraits, while in them the pilgrim, prioress-like conscious of the finer aspects of life, does deplore such matters as the Miller's indelicacy of language, contain a note of ungrudging admiration for efficient thievery. It is perhaps fortunate for the pilgrim's reputation as a judge of men that he sees through the Pardoner, since it is the Pardoner's particular tragedy that, except in Church, every one can see through him at a glance; but in Church he remains to the pilgrim "a noble ecclesiaste" (A 708). The equally repellent Summoner, a practicing bawd, is partially redeemed by his also being a good fellow, "a gentil harlot and a kynde" (A 647), and by the fact that for a moderate bribe he will neglect to summon: the pilgrim apparently subscribes to the popular definition of the best policeman as the one who acts the least policely.

Therefore Chaucer is tolerant, and has his little joke about the Summoner's small Latin—a very small joke, though one of the most amusing aspects of the pilgrim's character is the pleasure he takes in his own jokes, however small. But the Summoner goes too far when he cynically suggests that purse is the Archdeacon's hell, causing Chaucer to respond with a fine show of righteous respect for the instruments of spiritual punishment. The only trouble is that his enthusiastic defense of them carries *him* too far, so that after having warned us that excommunication will indeed damn our souls—

> But wel I woot he lyed right in dede:
> Of cursyng oghte ech gilty man him drede,
> For curs wol slee right as assoillyng
> savith—   A 661

he goes on to remind us that it will also cause considerable inconvenience to our bodies: "And also war hym of a *Significavit*" (A 662). Since a *Significavit* is the writ accomplishing the imprisonment of the excommunicate, the line provides perhaps the neatest—and most misunderstood—Chaucerian anticlimax in the Prologue.

I have avoided mentioning, hitherto, the pilgrim's reactions to the really good people on the journey—the Knight, the Parson, the Plowman. One might reasonably ask how his uncertain sense of values may be reconciled with the enthusiasm he shows for their rigorous integrity. The question could, of course, be shrugged off with a remark on the irrelevance to art of exact consistency, even to art distinguished by its verisimilitude. But I am not sure that there is any basic inconsistency. It is the nature of the pilgrim to admire all kinds of superlatives, and the fact that he often admires superlatives devoid of—or opposed to—genuine virtue does not inhibit his equal admiration for virtue incarnate. He is not, after all, a bad man; he is, to place him in his literary tradition, merely an average man, or mankind: *homo*, not very *sapiens* to be sure, but with the very best intentions, making his pilgrimage through the world in search of what is good, and showing himself, too frequently, able to recognize the good only when it is spectacularly so. Spenser's Una glows with a kind of spontaneous incandescence, so that the Red Cross Knight, mankind in search of holiness, knows her as good; but he thinks that Duessa is good, too. Virtue concretely embodied in Una or the Parson presents no problems to the well-intentioned observer, but in a world consisting mostly of imperfections, accurate evaluations are difficult for a pilgrim who, like mankind, is naïve. The pilgrim's ready appreciation for the virtuous characters is perhaps the greatest tribute that could be paid to their virtue, and their spiritual simplicity is, I think, enhanced by the intellectual simplicity of the reporter.

The pilgrim belongs, of course, to a very old—and very new—tradition of the fallible first person singular. His most exact modern counterpart is perhaps Lemuel Gulliver who, in his search for the good, failed dismally to perceive the difference between the pursuit of reason and the pursuits of reasonable horses: one may be sure that the pilgrim would have whinnied with the best of them. In his own century he is related to Long Will of *Piers Plowman*, a more explicit seeker after the good, but just as unswerving in his inability correctly to evaluate what he sees. Another kinsman is the protagonist of the *Pearl*, mankind whose heart is set on a transitory good that has been lost—who, for very natural reasons, confuses earthly with spiritual values. Not entirely unrelated is the protagonist of Gower's *Confessio Amantis*, an old man seeking for an impossible earthly love that seems to him the only good. And in more subtle fashion there is the teller of Chaucer's story of *Troilus and Cressida*, who, while not a true protagonist, performs some of the same functions. For this unloved "servant of the servants of love" falls in love with Cressida so persuasively that almost every male reader of the poem imitates him, so that we all share the heartbreak of Troilus and sometimes, in the intensity of our heartbreak, fail to learn what Troilus did. Finally, of course, there is Dante of the *Divine Comedy*, the most exalted member of the family and perhaps the immediate original of these other first-person pilgrims.

Artistically the device of the *persona* has many functions, so integrated with one another that to try to sort them out produces both oversimplification and distortion. The most obvious, with which this paper has been dealing—distortedly, is to present a vision of the social world imposed on one of the moral world. Despite their verisimilitude most, if not all, of the characters described in the Prologue are taken directly from stock and recur again and again in medieval literature. Langland in his own Prologue and elsewhere depicts many of them: the hunting monk, the avaricious friar, the thieving miller, the hypocritical pardoner, the unjust stewards, even, in little, the all-too-human nun. But while Langland uses the device of the *persona* with considerable skill in the conduct of his allegory, he uses it hardly at all in portraying the inhabitants of the social world: these are described directly, with the poet's own voice. It was left to Chaucer to turn the ancient stock satirical characters into real people assembled for a pilgrimage, and to have them described, with all their traditional faults upon them, by another pilgrim who records faithfully each fault without, for the most part, recognizing that it is a fault and frequently felicitating its possessor for possessing it. One result— though not the only result—is a moral realism much more significant than the literary realism which is a part of it and for which it is sometimes mistaken; this moral realism discloses a world in which humanity is prevented by its own myopia, the myopia of the describer, from seeing what the dazzlingly attractive externals of life really represent. In most of the analogues mentioned above the fallible first person receives, at the end of the book, the education he has needed: the pilgrim arrives somewhere. Chaucer never completed the *Canterbury Tales*, but in the Prologue to the *Parson's Tale* he seems to have been doing, rather hastily, what his contemporaries had done: when, with the sun nine-and-twenty degrees from the horizon, the twenty-nine pilgrims come to a certain—unnamed— *thropes ende* (I 12), then the pilgrimage seems no longer to have Canterbury as its destination, but rather, I suspect, the Celestial City of which the Parson speaks.

If one insists that Chaucer was not a moralist but a comic writer (a distinction without a difference), then the device of the *persona* may be taken primarily as serving comedy. It has been said earlier that the several Chaucers must have inhabited one body, and in that sense the fictional first person is no fiction at all. In an oral tradition of literature the first person probably always shared the personality of his creator: thus Dante of the *Divine Comedy* was physically Dante the Florentine; the John Gower of the *Confessio* was also Chaucer's friend John Gower; and Long Will was, I am sure, some one named William Langland, who was both long and wilful. And it is equally certain that Chaucer the pilgrim, "a popet in an arm t'enbrace" (B 1891), was in every physical respect Chaucer the man, whom one can imagine reading his work to a courtly audience, as in the portrait appearing in one of the MSS. of *Troilus*. One can imagine also the delight of the audience which heard the Prologue read in this way, and which was aware of the similarities and dissimilarities between Chaucer, the man before them, and Chaucer the pilgrim, both of whom they could see with simultaneous vision. The Chaucer they knew was physically, one gathers, a little ludicrous; a bourgeois, but one who was known as a practical and successful man of the court; possessed perhaps of a certain diffidence of manner, reserved, deferential to the socially imposing persons with whom he was associated; a bit absentminded, but affable and, one supposes, very good company—a good fellow; sagacious and highly perceptive. This Chaucer was telling them of another who, lacking some of his chief qualities, nevertheless possessed many of his characteristics, though in a different state of balance, and each one probably distorted just enough to become laughable without becoming unrecognizable: deference into a kind of snobbishness, affability into an over-readiness to please, practicality into Babbittry, perception into inspection, absence of mind into dimness of wit; a Chaucer acting in some respects just as Chaucer himself might have acted but unlike his creator the kind of man, withal, who could mistake a group of stock satirical types for living persons endowed with all sorts of superlative qualities. The constant interplay of these two Chaucers must have produced an exquisite and most ingratiating humor—as, to be sure, it still does. This comedy reaches its superb climax when Chaucer the pilgrim, resembling in so many ways Chaucer the poet, can answer the Host's demand for a story only with a rhyme he "lerned longe agoon" (B 1899)—*Sir Thopas*, which bears the same complex relation to the kind of romance it satirizes and to Chaucer's own poetry as Chaucer the pilgrim does to the pilgrims he describes and to Chaucer the poet.

Earlier in this paper I proved myself no gentleman (though I hope a scholar) by being rude to the Prioress, and hence to the many who like her and think that Chaucer liked her too. It is now necessary to retract. Undoubtedly Chaucer the man would, like his fictional representative, have found her charming and looked on her with affection. To have got on so well in so changeable a world Chaucer must have got on well with the people in it, and it is doubtful that one may get on with people merely by pretending to like them: one's heart has to be in it. But the third entity, Chaucer the poet, operates in a realm which is above and subsumes those in which Chaucer the man and Chaucer the pilgrim have their being. In this realm prioresses may be simultaneously evaluated as marvelously amiable ladies and as prioresses. In his poem the poet arranges for the moralist to define austerely what ought to be and for his fictional representative—who, as the representative of all mankind, is no mere fiction—to go on affirming affectionately what is. The two points of view, in strict moral logic diametrically opposed, are somehow made harmonious in Chaucer's wonderfully comic attitude, that double vision that is his ironical essence. The mere critic performs his etymological function by taking the Prioress apart and clumsily separating her good parts from her bad; but the poet's function is to build her incongruous and inharmonious parts into an inseparable whole which is infinitely greater than its parts. In this complex structure both the latent moralist and the naïve reporter have important positions, but I am not persuaded that in every case it is possible to determine which of them has the last word.[1]

---

[1] Quotations from Chaucer in this paper are made from F. N. Robinson's text (Cambridge, Mass., n.d.). Books referred to or cited are G. L. Kittredge, *Chaucer and His Poetry* (Cambridge, Mass., 1915), p. 45; Eileen Power, *Medieval People* (London, 1924), pp. 59–84. Robinson's note to A650 records the opinion that a *good felawe* means a "rascal." The medieval reader's expectation that the first person in a work of fiction would represent mankind generally and at the same time would physically resemble the author is commented on by Leo Spitzer in an interesting note in *Traditio*, IV (1946), 414–422. [For recent comment on this essay, see Major, "The Personality of Chaucer the Pilgrim," *PMLA*, LXXV (1960), 160 ff.—Ed.]

Ralph Baldwin

Chronology: Space-Time in the *Prologue*

Much scholarly effort has been devoted to demonstrating that the pilgrims themselves had prototypes in life, and there has been a further effort made to follow them on the road with an actual time table,[1] which would determine which tales were told, in what sequence, during which days of the pilgrimage. A careful scrutiny seems to reveal that the time element is one of the illusions of which Chaucer avails himself to give vraisemblance to the theme of pilgrimage. Though the spring is mentioned as a temporality, its relation to the traditions of beginning has been pointed out. Let us assume therefore that if the world began in the spring, it is reasonable enough for men to set out on a journey in the direction of holiness at that time. Any slight acquaintance with the mediaeval mind can account thus for April. No year is mentioned, no day is specified. The company is assembled by nightfall, a time at which inevitably travelers begin to gather at places of lodging.

We are precipitated into a beginning in time from the opening words, *Whan that,* which is associated with April, but which has in itself some of the suddenness of birth. The natural imagery following this introduction is less abrupt, conditioned as it is by such adjectives as *sote, swete, tendre, yonge.* And this renascence in nature is matched in human nature by an awakening sense of quest. Suddenly, in April, the sap moves, the birds sing, and mankind bestirs

itself for the journey to a far-off holy place.

A time factor enters in again with the not too precise dating, *in that seson* (1. 19), in April, with the sun halfway through the sign of the Ram . . . *on a day* (1. 19). It would be difficult to be more specific and less precise.

But though our time placement is nebulous, our position in space in these early lines is very clearly defined. We are in Southwark, at the Tabard, ready to join a pilgrimage, whose members do not themselves know yet that they are in Chaucer's party.

It is necessary here to point out that Chaucer has a dual role in the *Prologue* as well as in the tales themselves. This role of pilgrim and poet is obvious enough in the characterization and plot development of the links. In the *GP* there is an absolute separation of the function of poet and pilgrim, and it is here that we must consider the question of the relation of chronology to the whole of experience, for Chaucer the Poet obviously steps ahead of Chaucer the Pilgrim from the moment that the pilgrim narrator introduces his first traveling companion. Let us consider, at this juncture, the use made of tense to convey a kind of retrospective total acquaintance.

Every one of the pilgrims is introduced, uniformly, in the past tense: "A Knyght ther *was,*" "Ther *was* also a Nonne," and "The Millere *was* a stout carl," all past in terms of the auctorial present of the *story as it is being written.* But within the descriptive development of each character,

[1] Robert A. Pratt, "The Order of *The Canterbury Tales.*" *PMLA* LXVI (1951), 1141–1167.

Reprinted by permission of publisher and author from *The Unity of the Canterbury Tales,* Copenhagen, Rosenkilde and Bagger, 1955, pp. 54–57.

there are historically determined, or aoristic, or habitual employments of the past tenses, making for temporally rounded figures that are dramatically viable, but not too fixed to take on other nuances, other contours, during the progress of the cavalcade itself. The figures are not only depicted as past in respect to the pilgrimage, but there is a curious achronistic, placeless montage of past, present and future, on the one hand, and Tabard and road on the other. Whether by accident or design Chaucer, under the presumed duress of the speech situation as he companions with them at *that hostelry that night,* boldly arrogates to his characterizations information which he could only have come by after the party had taken to the road. The suffusion then of the static montage of the inn and the dynamic montage of the road in the *clause* of the *GP,* gives the illusion of the mobile wayfarer and the resident character. This is managed by Chaucer the Poet's telescoping several time continua and several space continua too, as he regards the situation from the vantage point of the prime mover or inventor of the pilgrimage.

The scene of meeting at the inn is a past definite. In introducing his new-found friends Chaucer suspends time—*er that I ferther in this tale pace*—and creates a kind of vacuum, a time-space continuum, in which he surveys his companions not as he sees them but as he will have seen them.

This *clause,* as Chaucer calls it, may be said to accomplish the pilgrimage by swinging it out of strict chronology and giving it a space-time *fiction* of its own. The illusion of wayfaring is created immediately in several ways, the most conspicuous of which is the casual interpolation emphasizing travel on horseback. If one considers the individual pilgrims one finds in the case of:

The Knight:

His hors were goode, but he was nat gay   A 74

and the verbs *ycome* (77) and *wente* (78) concluding his description.

The Squire:

Wel koude he sitte on hors and faire ryde   94

The Monk:

And whan he rood, men myghte his brydel heere   169

and

His bootes souple, his hors in greet estaat   203

and, the end line,

His palfrey was as broun as is a berye.   207

The Merchant:

In mottelee, and hye on horse he sat   271

The Clerk:

As leene was his hors as is a rake   287

The Sergeant of the Law:

He rood but hoomly in a medlee cote   328

The Shipman:

He rood upon a rouncy, as he kouthe   390

The Wife of Bath:

Upon an amblere esily she sat   469

. . . .

And on hir feet a paire of spores sharpe   473

The Plowman:

In a tabard he rood upon a mere.   541

The Miller:

A baggepipe wel koude he blowe and sowne,
And therwithal he broghte us out of towne.   566

The Reeve:

This Reve sat upon a ful good stot   615

. . . .

And evere he rood the hyndreste of oure route   622

The Somnour:

With hym ther rood a gentil Pardoner   669

The Pardoner:

Dischevelee, save his cappe, he rood al bare.   683

These lines serve to give a semblance of movement, of journey, of pilgrim progress anticipatorily, even before the leavetaking from the inn. In transfixing *travel* details to static *effictiones,* the character is broadened and enlivened proleptically with peculiar pilgrim intimations. These lines become, in short, metaphors for the pilgrimage motif. Chaucer is at pains in his *clause* to present a company of pilgrims on the road in the circumstances of travel.

The Tabard remains, to a certain extent, the permanent proscenium, even though in Chaucer the Pilgrim's time-table they leave it the next morning. Several of the vignettes, as is the case of the Prioress, are static rather than dynamic. The lengthy discussion of her table manners fixes her in the inn rather than on the road. And this association with food is used several times in other characterizations, notably the Monk's and the Franklin's, perhaps with the intention of reminding us that in point of true chronology we are at supper in the Tabard.

This Tabard-highroad tension creates a double illusion. It would seem that a deliberate bilocational, bifocal, and bitemporal effect is achieved by Chaucer. As a result, the fiction, by extension, moves on many levels, not the least of which is the bodying forth of the *vita est peregrinatio* motif in the timelessness of salvation. It is as if, even so early, we are asked to concede that:

> This world nys but a thurghfare ful of wo,
> And we been pilgrymes, passynge to and
> fro.   A 2848

Because the Christian, the pilgrim, moves in time and away from time, the consuming paradox of his nature, so Chaucer's pilgrims, ostensibly *en route*, have never left their hospice.

In the *Prologue*, although there are pilgrims, there is no pilgrimage—but there is a mighty illusion of one. Chaucer all but acknowledges that the reader has been taken in when he observes in the last section:

> And after wol I telle of our viage
> And al the *remenaunt* of our
> pilgrimage.   A 724

Kemp Malone

The Host

IN MY STUDY of the *Canterbury Tales* I have proceeded throughout on the presumption that Chaucer's pilgrims are fictitious, that they owe their existence to the workings of a great poet's imagination, and that they have no reality apart from the poem in which they appear. Modern researches into the background of Chaucer's life and writings, however, have unearthed various persons of flesh and blood who can be connected, more or less plausibly, with specific pilgrims in Chaucer's poem, and such connections have actually been made, notably by my revered master, the late John M. Manly, in his Lowell Institute lectures of 1924, later published in book form under the title *Some New Light on Chaucer*. What of these connections, and what bearing have they on our study of Chaucer's art? It will be convenient to approach this problem by a look at the host, a pilgrim who almost certainly had a counterpart in real life.

Chaucer gives the host special treatment in various ways which we need not go into here. For one thing, he tells us his full name. We have no such information about anybody else on the pilgrimage, apart from Chaucer himself. In the course of the narrative we learn the Christian names of eight other pilgrims, it is true. In the descriptions of the general prolog two such names are given: the prioress is called Eglentyne; the friar, Hubert. Later on, six other names appear: the miller is called Robin; the reeve, Oswald; the cook, Roger or Hodge; the monk, Piers; the nun's priest, John; and the wife of Bath, Alison or Alice. The remaining pilgrims go without names al-together; they are referred to exclusively as the knight, the squire, the man of law, and so on. The host's name, Harry Bailly, comes out in his quarrel with the cook; elsewhere he is called simply the host.

Now the records of the time show that there *was* an innkeeper of Southwark named Henry Bailly or Baillif. They do not tell us the name of the inn he kept, but the inference that he was the innkeeper of the Tabard seems plausible enough, and is generally made. Manly concludes (*op. cit.*, p. 83) that "the Host of the *Canterbury Tales* was modeled upon" the Henry Bailly that we know of from the historical records.

Even if this conclusion were correct it would not follow that the two Harry Baillies are to be identified. A work of art is one thing; its model in real life, something else again. The strictest of imitations does not reproduce the thing imitated. A copy always differs from its original. (These truisms Manly would of course agree with.) But evidence is wholly wanting that Chaucer's Harry Bailly had anything in common with the Harry Bailly of flesh and blood other than name, habitat, and occupation, three features not without importance but essentially external. Chaucer's characterization of the host reads thus:

A semely man our hoste was withalle
For to han been a marshal in an halle.
A large man he was, with eyen stepe,
A fairer burgeys is ther noon in Chepe:
Bold of his speche and wys and wel ytaught,
And of manhood him lakkede right naught.
Eek therto he was right a mery man.   A 757

Reprinted by permission of author and publisher from Kemp Malone, *Chapters on Chaucer*, Baltimore, The Johns Hopkins Press, 1951, pp. 186–197.

The superlative quality which we find in all the pilgrims appears again here, quite as one would expect, though the perfections of the host (as Chaucer is careful to tell us) befit not so much an innkeeper as a marshal. Such a host belongs to literature rather than to life, and in particular such a host belongs to the *Canterbury Tales,* where he fits well enough into the pattern of characterization regularly followed.

Nevertheless one cannot deny the possibility that the Harry Bailly of actual life was himself just such a person, however unlikely this may seem. Have we any evidence of Chaucer's intention in the matter? If he was intent on making a true portrait of a living model, if, as Edith Rickert puts it, he "had the habit of drawing his figures from the life" (*Chaucer's World,* p. 192), he would surely stick to the truth about his model, so far as he could. Now as it happens we know that the Harry Bailly of flesh and blood had a wife named Christian. In Chaucer, however, the host calls his wife not Christian but Godelief. Manly points this out and adds (*op. cit.,* p. 81),

What are we to say? It is possible, but hardly probable, that Godelief was Latinized in the record as Christian or that the English Godelief was used as a sort of bye-form of Christian. It is possible, of course, that the Christian of 1380 had died and that Harry Bailly had taken another wife by the time Chaucer had the Canterbury Tales in hand. And finally it is of course possible that Christian was still living but that Chaucer— although he calls her husband by his right name —preferred, for reasons best known to himself, not to use the right name of the wife.

Manly does not mention another possibility: that Chaucer, in giving to the host's wife the name Godelief, intended to distinguish his Harry Bailly from the Harry Bailly of actual life. But even this does not exhaust the possibilities. It seems to me quite possible that Chaucer did not know the actual Harry Bailly except by name, or that at any rate he did not know him well enough to know what his wife's name was. If so, the picture of the wedded pair, as well as the name of the wife, in the *Canterbury Tales* becomes essentially fictitious or imaginative, not a reproduction of the actual innkeeper of Southwark and his wife.

The passage in which the host's wife is characterized [in the Prologue of the *Monk's Tale*] has a special interest, not only for its own sake but also because it gives us a clue to Chaucer's choice of a name for the woman. . . . The host is here presented as a hen-pecked husband, a figure of fun, a comic character of ancient vintage, perennially amusing. His wife likewise is a character of broad comedy or farce: domineering, muscular, formidable beyond words, highly irascible, easily affronted, always looking for trouble and always making trouble for her unfortunate spouse. The name she bears, Godelief, that is, good and dear, is grotesquely at variance with her character, and thus adds to the comic or farcical effect.

The host has more to say about his wife in the epilog of the merchant's tale. . . . Here the host flatters himself that *his* wife is faithful to him, by way of contrast with the wife in the merchant's tale, who deceives *her* husband grossly. But fidelity seems to be the only virtue which the host's wife has. In this speech the host plays once again the part of the hen-pecked husband. He says he is afraid to make a clean breast of his domestic troubles, for fear some of the female pilgrims may tell his wife about it and bring another domestic storm down on his devoted head. But he has another reason for not going on with his sad story. His wife has so many vices that he can never hope to do justice to the subject; it would take a wit far greater than his to carry through so gigantic a task.

It will be seen that the host's wife, even though she is not one of the pilgrims, is characterized at some length, and in the usual superlatives. Chaucer puts the characterization in the husband's mouth, presumably for comic effect. The husband's confidence that his wife is faithful to him, whatever her faults may be, is doubtless meant to be funny, coming as it does immediately after May has convinced January of *her* fidelity in spite of the evidence of his own eyes. Certainly the rest of the host's speech about his wife is there to make us laugh. To me it seems wholly unlikely that Chaucer is giving us a true portrait of the wife of the actual Harry Bailly. The character of Godelief comes out of stock; every detail is conventional, and hoary with age. Godelief is a literary wife, not a wife of flesh and blood. And she is all the funnier for that.

As with the wife, so with the husband, even though he has his name in common with an actual innkeeper of Southwark. The host at every turn shows himself to be a character of fiction. His salient characteristic in the frame story is impudence, or "rude speech and bold," as Chaucer calls it. Such impudence as his belongs to broad comedy, in which servants habitually insult their masters and the masters take it with the utmost meekness. No such impudence befits an innkeeper in real life. The successful host in a tavern is commonly respectful to everybody, and particularly so to his betters. But *our* host plays a comic part, almost from the beginning. He bullies the pilgrims into taking him for guide and master of ceremonies; he brooks no opposition; he makes a point of being rude; he is highhanded at every turn. All this is meant to be funny. There is no realism about it; it is remote from the actualities of everyday existence.

One example of the host's behavior must suffice. The franklin is much impressed by the squire's tale, and by the personality of the squire, and he says so. He then goes on to speak of his own son, who has been a great disappointment to him:

> I have my sone snibbed, and yet shal,
> For he to vertu listeth nat entende;
> But for to pleye at dees, and to despende,
> And lese al that he hath, is his usage.
> And he hath lever talken with a page
> Than to comune with any gentil wight
> Ther he mighte lerne gentilesse aright.   F 694

At this point the host interrupts the franklin with the utmost rudeness:

> Straw for your gentilesse, quod our host;
> What, frankeleyn? pardee, sir, wel thou wost
> That eche of you mot tellen atte leste
> A tale or two, or breken his beheste.
> That knowe I wel, sir, quod the frankeleyn;
> I preye yow, haveth me nat in desdeyn
> Though to this man I speke a word or two.
> Telle on thy tale withouten wordes mo.
> Gladly, sir host, quod he, I wol obeye
> Unto your wil; now herkneth what I seye.
> I wol yow nat contrarien in no wyse
> As fer as that my wittes wol suffyse;
> I prey to god that it may plesen yow,
> Than woot I wel that it is good ynow.   F 706

Here the discourtesy of the host and the humble submission of the franklin are equally obvious and equally untrue to life. Note in particular the host's use of the lordly *thou*, and the franklin's response with the respectful *ye*. On an actual pilgrimage in fourteenth-century England this give and take would have been impossible: no innkeeper would have dreamt of behaving in this way towards a gentleman, and if he did so behave no gentleman would have put up with it. But in literature, and on the stage, the normal relationships of life may be, and often are, turned topsy-turvy for humorous purposes. The technic here used is that of broad comedy, with a deliberate and complete disregard for the realities of social intercourse.

The device which makes it possible for the host to behave as he does is explained in detail in the general prolog. Chaucer's account is humorous from start to finish, the host telling the pilgrims what to do and the pilgrims obeying his orders in comic reversal of the customary relationship between an innkeeper and his guests. The host begins by using a little flattery before bringing forward his proposal:

> Now, lordinges, trewely,
> Ye been to me right welcome hertely:
> For by my trouthe, if that I shal nat lye,
> I ne saugh this yeer so mery a companye

At ones in this herberwe as is now.
Fain wolde I doon yow mirthe, wiste I
  how.   A 766

Having opened the way by these words, he
makes his proposal, presenting it as an inspiration which has just come to him:

And of a mirthe I am right now bithought,
To doon yow ese, and it shal coste noght.
Ye goon to Caunterbury; god yow spede,
The blisful martir quyte yow your mede.
And wel I woot, as ye goon by the weye,
Ye shapen yow to talen and to pleye;
For trewely, confort ne mirthe is noon
To ryde by the weye doumb as a stoon;
And therfore wol I maken yow disport,
As I seyde erst, and doon yow som
  confort.   A 776

This is the proposal. You will note that the
host does not say what his scheme is. He
merely assures the pilgrims that it will give
them pleasure. And now he asks them to
take a vote on it:

And if yow lyketh alle, by oon assent,
Now for to stonden at my jugement,
And for to werken as I shal yow seye,
To-morwe, whan ye ryden by the weye,
Now, by my fader soule, that is deed,
But ye be merye, I wol yeve yow myn heed.
Hold up your hond, withouten more
  speche.   A 783

What are they to vote for? Not for any
particular scheme, since no scheme has
been laid before them. In effect, they are
asked to sign a blank cheque. They must
agree to do what the host tells them to do.
And the agreement must be unanimous.
Moreover, this action must be taken at once,
and without any discussion whatsoever.
Such a proposal seems a bit unreasonable,
but the pilgrims accept it without demur,
as they well might on an imaginary pilgrimage done in comic style, though hardly on
a pilgrimage in real life:

Our counseil was not longe for to seche;
Us thoughte it was nought worth to make it
  wys,
And graunted him withouten more avys,
And bad him seye his verdit as him
  leste.   A 787

The host now outlines his scheme for keeping the pilgrims occupied on the way to
Canterbury and back:

That ech of yow, to shorte with your weye,
In this viage, shal telle tales tweye,
To Caunterbury-ward, I mene it so,
And hom-ward he shal tellen other
  two, . . .   A 794

The scheme is obviously preposterous.
Picture in your mind's eye thirty-odd pilgrims on horseback, strung out for a quar-
ter of a mile on the Canterbury road, trying
to listen to one of their number who is
telling a tale as they ride along. How well
could they hear him? Those nearest to the
teller of the tale might hear much of it,
though even they would miss a good deal.
The rest of the pilgrims (by far the greatest
number) would hear nothing, or, at most,
would hear the speaker's voice without being able to make out the words. But did
any of the pilgrims point out this practical
difficulty, when the host made his proposal?
Not at all; they took it without a murmur.
They also accepted the host as their guide
and governor, and made no objection to
the huge fine which anyone who withstood
him was to pay:

Shal paye al that we spenden by the weye.
                                      A 806

In sum, the pilgrims took the host and his
nonsensical scheme without hesitation and
on his own terms. . . . Thenceforth the
host ruled the company of pilgrims; his
word was law, and his decisions prevailed.
And he did not hesitate to assert his authority. As Chaucer puts it,

He gan to speke as lordly as a king.   A 3900

This lordliness of his is of course meant
to be funny. A lordly innkeeper in the nature of the case is a comic figure.

The idea of putting an innkeeper at the
head of the group of pilgrims was one of
Chaucer's best inspirations. It gave rise to
a long series of amusing incidents in the
course of the pilgrimage, incidents which
could not have been staged had the knight

or one of the other "gentils" been put in command. The further idea of having the host *seize* the leadership was also a very happy one. The host took command in a highly amusing way, rushing the thing through so fast that the pilgrims had no time to consider what they were doing. One might say that the host used a kind of *blitz* technic in taking command. The absurdity of his program makes its adoption by the pilgrims much funnier than the adoption of a sensible program could possibly have been. And throughout the frame story the fun keeps up. The host proves a very fountain of merriment, one of the great comic characters of English literature. Besides, he is the link between the individual tales and the story of the pilgrimage. He makes the wheels go round. Through him a collection of tales becomes a unified work of art. Chaucer did not find such a character ready-made. The host is Chaucer's own creation, a figure of fiction, not a portrait of the actual innkeeper of Southwark.

But one may ask why Chaucer did not provide the host with a more reasonable scheme of story-telling than is the one which we find in the text. I have already tried to answer this question by pointing out that for Chaucer, bent on fun-making as he habitually was, the very absurdity of the program made it the right program, the one which had for him an irresistible appeal. This was the all-important consideration, but two things more may be said with some confidence. First and foremost, as we have already seen, Chaucer was not deeply concerned with plausibility or verisimilitude, whether in plot or in characterization. Secondly, when he decided to use the Canterbury pilgrimage for a frame he committed himself to a short journey and therefore had to use all his time for story-telling. Had the pilgrimage been one to Rome, say, he could have restricted the story-telling to overnight stops on the way, with the rout gathered about the speaker in conventional audience, but this procedure was not possible for a journey that lasted only three days. But what made him choose the Canterbury pilgrimage? Or, more precisely, what made him think of this pilgrimage? One can only guess that he had actually made the Canterbury pilgrimage himself and that his experiences as a pilgrim gave him the idea of using this pilgrimage as a frame. Certainly the Canterbury pilgrimage was deeply rooted in English life and this fact would surely have meant much to a man like Chaucer.

George Lyman Kittredge

The Shipman and the Prioress

THE SHIPMAN'S TALE was originally intended for a woman; for the Wife of Bath, beyond a doubt. It accords with her character both in style and in sentiment. Its tone is hers precisely, frankly sensual,—unmoral, if you like,—but too hearty and too profoundly normal to be unwholesome. And there are many expressions in the story which were clearly written for her and for her alone.

The tale turns upon a trick by which a rich merchant was cheated out of a sum of money by Dan John, a monk, with certain incidental deceptions which we may ignore. The Wife of Bath knew many merchants. As a maker of cloth, she had, quite possibly, recollections not altogether pleasant of her dealings with such personages, though we may feel pretty confident that they had seldom got ahead of her in a bargain. But Chaucer changed his plan, and it is vastly interesting to see his masterpiece gradually taking shape as he goes on with it. Even as he wrote the tale of Dan John and the merchant, the Wife of Bath's character grew upon him. He conceived the happy idea of devoting a whole act of his Human Comedy to the discussion of Marriage, and he saw that nobody could be so well fitted as the Wife to precipitate such a discussion, and to control it while it lasted. With this in view, he furnished her with a succession of five husbands, and with a monstrously heretical tenet as to the Subjection of Men. This development of his plan released the story of Dan John and the merchant, and Chaucer assigned it to the Shipman, to whom it was almost as appropriate. For our master mariner was engaged in the foreign trade, and had no objection to satirizing the merchants who chartered his barge, the Maudlin. Indeed, he used to take large toll from the cargo, when that consisted of wine:—

> Ful many a draught of wyn hadde he ydrawe
> From Bordeaux-ward, whil that the chapman sleep.
> Of nice conscience took he no keep.   A 398

Of course, the presence of a substantial and very dignified merchant among the Pilgrims gave special zest, for both Wife and Shipman, to the telling of this particular tale.

Here we have again a trait of Chaucer's method, or, let us rather say, another proof of his fruitful observation of life. An anecdote always gains point if there is somebody present whom it may be thought to hit. Again and again is this principle expressly recognized by the Canterbury Pilgrims. The Miller's Tale concerns a carpenter, and the Reeve, who is of that trade, suspects that it is aimed at him:—

> "This dronke miller hath ytold us heer
> How that bigyled was a carpenter,
> Peraventure in scorn, for I am oon;
> But, by your leve, I shal him quyte
> anoon."   A 3916

And so the saturnine Oswald returns the compliment in a tale of a miller. The Cook's Tale, fortunately a fragment, was to be of an innkeeper, and was avowedly a reply to the Host's attack upon the artifices of chefs and caterers. The Friar and the Sumner

Reprinted by permission of the publishers from George Lyman Kittredge, *Chaucer and His Poetry*, Cambridge, Mass., Harvard University Press, 1915, 1946, pp. 170–180.

furnish a similar comic interlude at each other's expense. All these are obvious and familiar instances; but what is expressly stated in these cases, we are left to extend, when we see occasion, to other tales, as well as to the conversation of the Pilgrims. And this story of the Shipman's is a case in point. Indications are abundant, as any one may see for himself by comparing the character of the Merchant in the general prologue with the words and demeanor of the merchant in the Shipman's Tale. One passage is enough for my purpose. Says the Shipman's merchant:

"Wyf," quod this man, "litle canstow devyne
The curious bisinesse that we have.
For of us chapmen, al-so God me save
And by that lord that cleped is Seint Yve!
Scarsly amonges twelve, ten shul thryve,
Continuelly, lastinge un-to our age.
We may wel make chere and good visage,
And dryve forth the world as it may be,
And kepen our estaat in privetee,
Til we be deed, *or elles that we pleye*
A pilgrimage, or goon out of the weye.
And therfor have I greet necessitee
Up-on this queinte world tavyse me;
For evermore we mote stonde in drede
Of hap and fortune in our
    chapmanhede."   B 1428

When this was uttered, did not every man and woman in the company look at the Merchant? "Perhaps," they thought, "he too is playing a pilgrimage to dodge his creditors." But they could not believe such a thing.

There wiste no man that he was in dette,
So estatly was he of his governaunce.   A 281

Chaucer does not know that he is in debt either. He merely suggests it as a possibility, as something incident to a merchant's life.

Now the Shipman's Tale is not merely a jest at the expense of merchants. It touches up the monks as well. Dan John was, in rank and station, just such a man as the Monk of the Pilgrimage. Both were persons of position in their order, often en-

trusted with important business by their abbot. Chaucer's Monk is expressly called an "out-rider," and the Shipman's Dan John received a commission from his superior to "ride out"—that is, to make a tour of inspection in regard to the remoter farms and rented properties of the monastery. The Host receives the story with loud acclaim, and exhorts the company to heed the moral:—"Aha, fellows! be on your guard against such tricks. Don't invite any monks to visit your houses." Naturally, he points his remarks by a look or a gesture, so as to raise a laugh at the stately Monk who is riding among the Pilgrims on his berry-brown palfrey, with bridle jingling as loud and clear as the chapel-bell. And later, when he calls on him for a story in his turn, he alludes with sufficient definiteness to the Shipman's fabliau, even asking him if his name is not likewise Dan John. The Prioress is listening, and when, in her tale of the murdered little boy, she has occasion to mention an abbot who was true to his sacred office and had the grace of God to work a miracle, she cannot ignore the Host's gibe. "This abbot," says the Prioress,—

"This abbot, which that was a holy man,
As monkes been—or elles oughten be."   B 1833

And again: "This holy man, this abbot, him mene I." This is not satire; it is a tribute, rather, which may serve to correct the Host for his flippancy without being precisely a rebuke. There may be bad monks in the world; but the Prioress has no personal knowledge of any such, and is not disposed to lend an ear to current slander.

Of all the Canterbury Pilgrims none is more sympathetically conceived or more delicately portrayed than Madame Eglantine, the prioress. The impression she has made upon the company is exquisitely suggested by the courtesy with which the Host invites her to tell a story after the Shipman has finished. His softness of speech and manner contrasts strongly with the robust badinage that immediately precedes.

"Wel sayd, by corpus dominus!" quod our
    hoste,
"Now longe moote thou saile by the coste,
Sire gentil master, gentil marineer!
God yeve this monk a thousand last quad yeer!
Aha, felawes! beth war of swich a iape.
The monk putte in the mannes hood an ape,
And in his wyves eek, by seynt Austyn.
Draweth no monkes more unto your in.
But now passe over, and lat us seke aboute,
Who shal now telle first, of al this route,
Another tale," and with that word, he seyde.
As curteysly as it hadde been a mayde:
"My lady Prioresse, by your leve,
So that I wiste I sholde you nat greve,
I wolde demen that ye tellen sholde
A tale next, if so were that ye wolde.
Now, wol ye vouchesaf, my lady deere?"
"Gladly," quod she, and seyde as ye shal
    here.   B 1642

The Prioress is of noble blood, and has
been brought up from youth in a religious
order; but it is a rich order, of the kind
to which parents of wealth and position
entrusted, as they still entrust, their daugh-
ters for care and education. She travels in
modest state, with a nun for her secretary,
and three attendant priests, who suffice on
occasion to guard her from unpleasant contact with the rougher elements in the company. But her gentleness and sweet dignity
are her best protection. She lives, as it were,
in a cloister, even on the road to Canterbury. Yet she does not hold herself aloof.
She is fond of society and shows no stiffness
of demeanor. Her conversational talents are
particularly insisted on. She is excellent
company—"of great desport"—and very
pleasant and amiable in her demeanor.

She peyned her to countrefete chere
Of court, and been estatlych of manere.   A 140

This couplet is often sadly misunderstood,
as if the Prioress's bearing were a labored
and affected imitation of polite behavior.
It implies merely that her manners were
exquisitely courtly, with that little touch
of preciseness and finish which shows that
one regards such things as of some concern.
Her position in life required this of her,

and it accorded with her nature as well. As
to her table manners, which often make the
uninstructed laugh, they are simply the
perfection of mediaeval daintiness. Nothing
is farther from Chaucer's thought than to
poke fun at them. Her greatest oath (for in
those days everybody swore) was "by St.
Loy." Could there be a sweeter or more
ladylike expletive? It is soft and liquid,
and above all, it does not distort the lips.
Her little dogs went with her on the journey, and she watched over them with anxious affection:—

Sore weep she if oon of hem were deed,
Or if men smote it with a yerde smerte.   A 149

It is no accident that Chaucer makes her
tell the infinitely pathetic legend of the
pious little boy who was murdered for his
childlike devotion to the Blessed Virgin.
"This little child," she calls him, "learning
his little book, as he sat in the school at
his primer."

This litel child, his litel book lerninge,
As he sat in the scole at his primer,
He Alma Redemptoris herde singe
As children lerned here antiphoner.
And, as he dorste, he drough him neer and
    neer,
And herkned ay the wordes and the note
Til he the firste vers coude al by rote.

Noght wiste he what this Latyn was to seye,
For he so yong and tendre was of age.
But, on a day, his felawe gan he preye,
T' expounen him this song in his langage,
Or telle him why this song was in usage:
This preyd he him to constrewe and declare
Ful ofte tyme upon his knowes bare.

His felawe, which that elder was than he,
Answerde him thus: "This song, I have herd
    seye,
Was maked of our blisful lady free,
Hire to salewe, and eek hire for to preye
To been our help and socour whan we deye:—
I can no moore expoune in this matere—
I lerne song—I can but smal grammere."

"And is this song maked in reverence
Of Cristes moder?" seyde this innocent.
"Now, certeyn, I wol do my diligence

To conne it al, er Cristemasse is went:
Though that I for my prymer shal be shent,
And shal be beten thryes in an houre,
I wol it conne, our lady for to
    honoure!"   B 1733

His mother looked for him at night, but
he did not come home, and she sought him
everywhere—"with modres pitee in her
brest enclosed." What can the Prioress
know of a mother's feelings? Everything,
though she is never to have children, having
chosen, so she thought, the better part. But
her heart goes out, in yearnings which she
does not comprehend or try to analyze, to
little dogs, and little boys at school. Nowhere is the poignant trait of thwarted
motherhood so affecting as in this character
of the Prioress.

You do not care to hear from me that
Geoffrey Chaucer took pleasure in birds
and flowers and running brooks, that he
loved the sunshine on the grass or as it
streamed through storied windows, that it
was a delight to him to walk in the dewy
rides of the king's forest and see buck and
doe and fawn in the distance, or watch the
squirrels scamper up the beeches and spring
from branch to branch and sit looking at
him with their little beady eyes—

The many squirreles, that sete
Ful hye upon the trees, and ete,
And in here maner maden festes.   *B. D.* 433

Nor do you care to hear of his worship of
"these flowers white and red, such as men
callen daisies in our town."

These things are amiable and charming,
but they are matters of every day. The supreme genius knows how to seize the moment of intensest self-revelation for each
of his characters; and then, a phrase will
do the business. It may be Menelaus to
Helen, in Euripides:—"Leave you in
Egypt! It was for you that I sacked Troy."
Or Falstaff, musing as he grows old:—
"O, it is much that a lie with a slight oath,
and a jest with a sad brow, will do with a
fellow that never had the ache in his shoul-
ders." Or Lady Macbeth:—"Here's the
smell o' the blood still. All the perfumes of
Arabia will not sweeten this little hand."
And so in Chaucer—there is the Wife of
Bath, hugging to her tough old heart the
remembrance of her "world" that she has
had "in her time." There is Cressida, false
to the matchless Troilus, but promising herself to be faithful to her new lover—"To
Diomede, algate, I wol be trewe"; and the
Pardoner, the one lost soul among the Canterbury Pilgrims: "Christ grant you his
pardon! I will not deceive you. God knows
it is better than mine"; and Madame Eglantine the holy nun, with her pious legend of
the little boy learning his little book.

Dale Underwood

The First of *The Canterbury Tales*

THERE was a time when one might have presented a new interpretation of the "Knight's Tale" under the species of title still employed by the Miltonists for that "two-handed engine"—for example, "The Knight's Tale Again" or "The Realm of Theseus Revisited." But by now there has been such a crush of revisitations and such a bewildering disparity of consequences that one Chaucerian has, out of his distress, issued a polite but firm remonstrance entitled "Knight's Tale, 38." [1] It might henceforth be assumed that only the very brave or very foolish would dare to venture forth with Version 39. My strategy in making that venture is to disclaim membership in either of these classes by professing the role of mediator: I offer my own "variant reading" as a measure of reconcilement among precedent and conflicting views.

Of relatively recent studies, Charles Muscatine's essay, "Form, Texture, and Meaning in Chaucer's 'Knight's Tale,' " seems to me especially significant. [2] But in some fundamental respects its insights, I think, should be extended and revised. And one line of revision looks toward those readers who have believed, on a variety of grounds, that the Tale depicts its human world in a more critical light than Muscatine's view and most of those before it will allow.

In the terms of Muscatine's study, the Tale is essentially "a poetic pageant" designed to express "the nature of the noble life." More specifically, the essay proposes that "order, which characterizes the framework of the poem, is also at the heart of its meaning"; that the extensive and formal description, the deliberate pace, the marked and pervasive symmetry of movement and structure, are expressive of the pageantry, nobility, and order; that "the society depicted is one in which form is full of significance . . . and wherein life's pattern is itself a reflection, or better, a reproduction of the order of the universe." As a consequence of all this, the "noble" order of the poem's form is to be viewed as expressing the noble order of the life depicted. And we may assume then, though the essay does not explicitly make this extension, that the order of the poem expresses also the order of the universe.

Falling across this "pattern of order," however, is the "constant awareness of a formidably antagonistic element—chaos, disorder." More specifically still, a "tension" exists "between the poem's symmetrically ordered structure and the violent ups and downs of the surface narrative." This tension expresses the conflict between order and disorder, in which the "patterned edifice of the noble life" stands as a "bulwark" against the "ever-threatening forces of chaos, and in constant collision with them." Accordingly, "the real moral issue of the poem" lies in the clash of these two forces, and in the consequent nature of man's relation to the universe.

The terms and concepts involved in this reading focus, I believe, upon the most essential aspects of the Tale. Yet they seem susceptible of fuller and more precise con-

[1] Edward B. Ham, "Knight's Tale, 38," *ELH*, XVII (1950), 252–261.
[2] *PMLA*, LXV (1950), 911–929.

Reprinted by permission of author and editor from *ELH*, XXVI (1959), 455–469.

tent than they have been given. And when we have supplied this content, we may see that the actual form and meaning of the poem are significantly different from those envisioned by the essay.

We may begin by noting that the most obvious and striking principle of *order* in the poem's *form* derives precisely from what Muscatine has called the "violent ups and downs" which distinguish the "surface narrative." In other words, the most conspicuous characteristic of the world with which the poem deals is one of mutability, transmutation, and incessant fluctuation between radically juxtaposed extremes. This principle is implicit in the opening lines of the Tale; and from there it steadily expands in operation and meaning. In the first five lines of the Tale, we are told that once, long ago, Theseus was not only "lord and governour" of Athens, but "in his time" the greatest conqueror "under the sunne." The implications of Theseus' position—under the sun and in time—begin immediately to unfold in both theme and rhythmic pattern. Through the swift summary of Theseus' ventures in "Femenye," which comes immediately after the opening lines, we learn that his war with the Amazons is followed by his wedding with their queen; and that the feast at his wedding is followed by the tempest at his homecoming. Then, in the first event of the narrative proper, his triumphant approach to Athens, "In al his wele and in his mooste pride" (895) is abruptly confronted by the suppliant ladies in all their woe and lamentation. Next, as the consequence of this confrontation, the city of Thebes is totally destroyed, and the "bones" of the ladies' husbands "restored" (991–92). Finally—as conclusion to this opening phase of the poem, which serves as prelude to the rest—the "joye" and "honour" of the conqueror at his second homecoming is immediately juxtaposed with the "angwissh" and "wo" of Palamon and Arcite in the conqueror's prison (1028–30).

This principle of order in the form and movement of the poem pervades every aspect of its structure. The radiant May garden, in which the more radiant Emelye sings like an "aungel," is "evene joynant" to the gloomy "dongeoun" of the prison where Palamon and Arcite "compleyn" (1051–72). Similarly, at the end of Pt. I both Palamon and Arcite are in despair— the one because he is in prison, and the other because he is out. But at the end of Pt. II they are both of "herte blithe" because the "noble" Theseus has granted them "so fair a grace" (1874–78)—namely, permission "to fighte for a lady, benedicitee!" (2115). Again—as the consequence of this permission, and as the two major events in Pt. IV preceding the resolution of the narrative—the proud pageantry of the lists, in which the mighty Theseus sits "as he were a god in trone" (2529), is followed by the mournful pageantry of Arcite's funeral, with Theseus weeping piteously over the dead body.

It must be apparent that while this pattern constitutes a basic principle of order in the form of the poem, it appears in its "ups and downs" to express for the world depicted a continual source and principle of disorder—not only of instability, transiency, and flux, but of repeated frustration, *renversement,* and woe. It is in essence, and when viewed in itself, the world seen under the aspect of Fortune, as described in Bk. II of Boethius' *Consolation of Philosophy.* Yet the seeming disorderliness of life which this view involves does not consist in chaos or disorder per se, but in the superimposition of a non-human logic and order upon the attempted order of human thought and aspiration. For, despite the human malice which the Middle Ages commonly attributed to Fortune, her logic is essentially non-human because it is mechanical. Its principle of order is the incessant turn of the wheel.

Accordingly, those aspects of the poem's order by which this principle is expressed assume themselves an element of the mechanical. We know, for example, that the Knight, as he so consciously orders his tale, is perpetually and deliberately "turning"— now on the one side to take up Arcite, then "Upon that oother syde Palamon" (1275), and so on through the narrative of the poem. In the world of the poem, in turn, this principle of mechanical order extends not merely to the "fortunes" of the characters, but to their nature and behavior as well. Thus the fluctuating moods of the lover Arcite in his grove are "Now up now doun, as boket in a welle" (1533). One consequence of this principle is that, in terms of human logic and order, the nature of man himself becomes a continual source of apparent disorder.

But the principle of mechanical order is not, of course, the only one in the poem. There is also in the poem's form and world the principle of human order. Unlike the first, this order—as the product of the human mind and will—is purposive rather than mechanical. Its purpose is the fulfillment of human nature as conceived by the human mind. And it seeks to move toward that fulfillment by harmonizing the diverse forces within man and those which, as he conceives them, operate upon him from without. Its aim, in one sense, is stability rather than incessant change, and, in another sense, development rather than repetition. Iconically, therefore, its chief figurations are, first, a purposely fixed and unified design of diverse parts, rather than unpurposive fluctuation between discordant extremes; and, second, a progressive movement of line, rather than a closed circle. This principle of human order, while antithetical to the order of the mechanical, seeks to transcend it by accommodating it to human design and progression.

In the formal cause of the poem, this situation is vested in the Knight. While in telling his narrative he is constantly "turning," he is at the same time purposely constructing a design which is more than the turn of the wheel. And within this design,

the panoply of war, the anatomy of love, the ceremony of death assume their fixed places in the symmetrically balanced show of life as the Knight, with his own human logic and order, conceives it. But our present concern is with the principle of human order as it operates in the world depicted by the Tale. And there its most triumphant expression stands at the center of the poem.

The lists described at the beginning of Pt. III are, of course, built by Theseus in his attempt as "lord and governour" to bring human order out of disorder—to resolve the enmity and strife which have arisen between two previously sworn brothers in their desire to win the same woman. In themselves the lists, or what the poem calls the "noble theatre" (1885), created by Theseus are not only the perfect expression of human order as conceived by their maker; they are his little world, his "O." And when he had created it, "hym lyked wonder weel" (2092). But his little world was also a circle. And this perfect expression of human order or "art" was also filled with disorder—not only in the portraiture of the gods whom this creator "under the sun" served, but in the "noble" battle with which this little world was presently to be filled. And in both situations—if I may resort to the handbook of current literary criticism—the relation of human order to disorder seems paradoxical, ironical, ambiguous, and ambivalent. The relationship is also, I believe, an essential key not only to the form and meaning of the "Knight's Tale," but to the thought and art of Chaucer.

In the little world created by Theseus, the disorder—in both the portraiture of the gods and the "noble" battle of the lists—is revealed through human art or order. That is to say both that the disorder is converted to order and that the order has within itself disorder. And this situation defines, in turn, the human world of the poem. For while the human order in that world does in part express wisdom, strength, and nobility, it at the same time expresses blindness, weakness, and "wrecchednesse." And since this situation seems to me most crucially vested in Theseus, I shall focus primarily upon him.

In the series of cumulative actions and decisions which Theseus takes, it is significant that we begin with Thebes. We at once recall the beginning of the *Roman de Thèbes:* Laius' attempt to preserve his life and the order of his kingdom by murdering his son; and the son, after the unwitting murder of his father, solving in his human wisdom the riddle of the Sphinx and, as human reward for his victory, marrying his mother and further damning the city which he attempts to save. Theseus' destruction of Thebes at once completes and extends the pattern. His action thereby places itself and all that emerges in the poem (and, I believe, in varying ways all that emerges in *The Canterbury Tales*) in a vast and continuing perspective of human action and destiny. To preserve human order, nobility, dignity, justice, and mercy—and, in the shadow of Oedipus, to preserve also his role, honor, and glory as the greatest conqueror under the sun—he destroys a great city of thousands to avenge the wrong done to a "compaignye of ladyes" (898).

This initial action of the "noble duc" triggers, if I may, the series that follows in the Tale. For this series of actions, which constitutes the "progressive line" in the principle of human order, becomes at the same time an increasing line of disorder. Two sworn brothers, who had nothing to do with the offense to the ladies and who survive the destroyed city of Thebes, are transplanted now to Athens, the realm of Theseus, where they are cast "in prisoun perpetuelly" and with "no raunsoun" (1023–24) by this temporal lord and governor—and, therefore, the temporal officer of justice and mercy. Under the office of Venus, they fall into bitter enmity over a girl who knows nothing about the situation and who wishes to remain a virgin under

the office of Diana. One is released from this prison of Theseus, while the other is not, because he is a friend of a friend of the temporal lord. Under the office of Mars they fight, ankle-deep in blood, a duel for love. This leads, through the judgment and "grace" of the temporal lord, to a far more sanguinary battle involving two hundred of the best knights of the land and fought under the auspices now of three gods, Venus, Mars, and Diana. This leads, in turn, to the human victor's being deprived of his reward and his life. He is deprived of them through the office and judgment of Saturn, the avowed god of disorder—who stands, like Venus, Mars, and Diana, midway in power and station between the temporal lord and the "First Mover" to whom we shall presently turn. The human victor is deprived of his life and his humanly just rewards apparently so that order may be "restored" by the god of disorder in the middle realm of godhood. And in all this, the god of disorder stands at the apex of his group as Theseus stands at the apex of his—Palamon, Arcite, and Emelye—in the realm of man.

The departures from the *Teseide* which Chaucer made in developing this line of action seem to me important in determining its significance. The fact of Thebes' destruction, for example, may have been taken from the *Roman de Thèbes.* But we must ask why in Chaucer's poem it takes place *after* Theseus has slain Creon, who was alone responsible for the offense to the ladies. Similarly we must ask why, in mentioning that Theseus "dide with al the contree as hym liste" (1004), Chaucer substituted a pillage of the dead and wounded for the more humane and orderly conduct related by Boccaccio. The events as narrated in the "Knight's Tale" undoubtedly reflect practices of Chaucer's time. But the fact that they do so is a part of the point I wish to make. For their very typicality stresses the paradoxical and cumulative elements of order and disorder in the principle of human order which Theseus represents.[3]

This situation is continued in subsequent modifications. In the narrative line of the poem, Theseus' pivotal decisions stand at the center. In forgiving his "mortal enemies," Palamon and Arcite (see 1724, 1736, 1794), Theseus exercises mercy over justice, "resoun" over "ire" (1765–66), pity over hate. And his sense of absurdity in the situation of the two young knights as lovers serves as a further testimony of his maturity and wisdom. But it serves at the same time to question the wisdom of his solution. The resort to combat and the construction of the lists involved were again, of course, thoroughly typical of the chivalric order in Chaucer's time. Yet we know also that they both represented practices which were items of public controversy.[4] It is difficult to assume, therefore, that in having Theseus enlarge upon the folly— however typically human—of their cause, Chaucer was unaware that he was thereby stressing the problematic character of Theseus' own human decisions and actions.

By introducing the role of Saturn into the poem, Chaucer seems to me to continue this line of development while climactically articulating some related problems. At his fictive surface, Saturn represents a force of disorder external and superior to the human world of the poem. And the decision which he makes thus seems not only a devastating frustration of Theseus' attempt at justice and order but a reduction of the human world to a helpless victim of whimsical forces beyond its control. We are obliged to ask, therefore, what real order if any there is in the universe and how that order, if it exists, is related to the order of man. But at the end of the poem Theseus'

own statements regarding the order of the "First Mover" specifically oblige us to consider the significance of Saturn's position within that order—that is, beneath the First Mover and above Theseus' position as temporal lord. And within this line of descent we are to see, I think, that as a universal force Saturn is in one sense external and superior to the human world, but in another sense the reflection of a force which is part of the nature of man. Consequently while Theseus reflects the order of the First Mover, he also reflects the disorder of Saturn.

As the climactic point both in Chaucer's departures from the *Teseide* and in the poem as a whole, Theseus' final speech sustains this interpretation. For within that speech the temporal lord perfectly exemplifies his human nobility, dignity, wisdom, attempt at order, and quite justified belief that in all this he and his world are at once a part and a reflection of the order which is divine. But he also fails perfectly to see the precise and most crucial ways in which this is true. And, again in the shadow of Oedipus, he has not seen in the very act of seeing why he should not see. Let me explain.

Following the death and funeral of Arcite, Theseus' final speech offers his world in two quite literal senses the "consolation of philosophy." In the history of western thought—as distinct for the moment from the dramatic context of the poem—the specific ideas which Theseus expounds had, of course, been familiar before Boethius wrote his own *Consolation.* And their historical commonness is entirely relevant to the role and final speech of Theseus in the "Knight's Tale." But we may be sure that the poem is specifically mindful of Boethius' *Consolation,* and with significance beyond the mere currency of its thought, when we consider how Theseus' speech completes and climaxes a pattern of ideas which bear upon Boethius' work.

[3] See Henry J. Webb, "A Reinterpretation of Chaucer's Theseus," *RES*, XXIII (1947), 289–296, for a further discussion of some of the questions here raised regarding Theseus' role in the poem.
[4] See G. R. Owst, *Literature and Pulpit in Medieval England* (Cambridge, 1933), 334–336 and passim.

At the end of Pt. I, Arcite's lament—prompted by his release from Theseus' prison and his banishment from sight of Emelye—questions the wisdom and order of man. And in doing so it echoes the wisdom of Dame Philosophy in Bk. III of the *Consolation*. This is at once followed, "upon that oother syde," by Palamon's lament, which is prompted by his not being released from Theseus' prison and which, echoing the complaint of Boethius in Bk. I, questions the wisdom and order of the divine. In the final or fourth part of the Tale, Egeus' consolation to his son echoes Dame Philosophy in Bk. II. It accepts, rather than questions, the human situation. But it does so simply in terms of the world's mutability —in other words, with the world seen essentially as under the aspect or order of Fortune, and therefore as "a thurghfare ful of wo." But Theseus' following consolation, at the conclusion of the Tale, draws upon the wisdom of Dame Philosophy in Bks. II, III, and IV, though it is primarily anchored in the last of these. And like Egeus, Theseus also accepts rather than questions the human situation—but now under the order of the divine.

This pattern of progressive order in the poem thus corresponds to the pattern of progressive order in Boethius' *Consolation*. But while Theseus' wisdom omits the questioning of divine order at the beginning of that work, it also omits the acceptance in the fifth and last book of man's own free will and responsibility for his fate—in other words, of man's reponsibility for his own realm or level of human order. Theseus' consolation to his world, then, while resting on the middle portion of Boethius' *Consolation,* omits the lowest and the highest reaches of that work's progressive view by omitting its beginning and end. Further, though the highest reach of Theseus' wisdom stops at Bk. IV, he sees—like Troilus in his use of Bk. V—only a portion of his text. An essential cause of this situation in both instances is made clear by Dame Philosophy when she tells her human pa-tient that the higher or more "deeply penetrating" views of Bks. IV and V are "almost impossible" even for her adequately to attain. Consequently the human reason can only reach toward but never fully comprehend the nature and purpose of the divine will and order or its relationship to the will and order of man. The partial blindness and, therefore, seeming disorder in all human wisdom, experience, and attempt at order is a necessary consequence. This returns us to what has repeatedly, and in its proper sense justly, been called the human nobility and maturity of Theseus' speech.

In terms now of philosophic system rather than the dramatic structure of Boethius' work, what Theseus sees in a sense is the top and bottom of the divine order, but not the middle where he himself belongs. He sees that Nature has taken its beginning from a thing stable and eternal and that, while in its diversity of things, it is bound by the great chain of love, it descends till it becomes "corrumpable" (3010); that, as a result all things born in "this wrecched world adoun" must die (2995); that this, too, is part of the divine order; and that here, as throughout, the "First Mover" is

Convertynge al unto his propre welle
From which it is dirryved, sooth to telle.   3038

What Theseus does not see are the full implications of Nature's descent to corruptibility. More precisely, he does not see the position and role of human order, which stands in the middle of the descent—that is, between the order of mutability in Fortune and the stability of the First Mover. More precisely still, he does not see—as Dame Philosophy sees in Boethius' Bk. IV—that, standing in the middle of Nature's descent into corruptibility, he is not, like Fortune, totally blind but partially so. And in this partial blindness, he does not see—as Dame Philosophy sees in Boethius' Bk. V—that he has, nevertheless, a free will and, therefore, responsibility for his actions in this human world of which he is "lord and governour." In sum, he fails to see the essential crux of the human situation. And the crux is not only that, though partially blind, man is responsible for his destiny; it is also that this apparent disorder and injustice in terms of human logic is part of the logic, justice, and order of the divine, operating in time and under the sun.

Faced, accordingly, with the fact of Arcite's death at the end of the poem, the "wise" Theseus can only conclude that since as part of the divine order all things born must die, his human world must "maken vertu of necessitee" (3042) and rejoice that Arcite has escaped "Out of this foule prisoun of this lyf" (3061). He has not seen that his own will, judgment, and attempt at order have contributed to that death. Nor has he seen that his placing Arcite in his own prison without "raunsoun" at the beginning of the poem has contributed to the unfolding line of human disorder which, now at the poem's end, seems to have reduced his world itself to a "wrecched" one and a "foule prisoun." Finally, he has not seen that this particular descent in the corruptibility of human nature and order is itself at once a part and a reflection of that general descent in Nature which he has himself defined. And he has not seen all this because, as part of the human world under the sun, he is himself "corrumpable."

The poem, however, does see all this. And at what I think we must now call its divine level of order, the "seer" and maker is no longer Theseus or the Knight, but the poet who conceives and makes them both. The poem is finally, then, the poet's theatre, world, and tale, in which he images the form and principle not only of Fortune and of man but, encompassing and transcending these, the universe of divine order. But unlike the principle of human order, which reveals its disorder through apparent order, this divine world reveals its order through apparent disorder. This is in part to say that its logic, like the order of Fortune, is non-human. But it is so because it is super-human and, therefore, in the words of Dame Philosophy, "almost impossible" for the human mind to comprehend. Again like the principle of Fortune, and unlike the principle of human order, its executing movement in time and things is cyclical. But unlike Fortune and like the order of man, this movement is at the same time a progressive and unfolding line.[5] And this returns us to the embodied world of the Tale.

We know that the Tale begins with two mighty battles of the greatest conqueror under the sun and ends with the quiet and humble marriage of a man and woman. The line of narrative action by which the beginning and end are joined is also the progressive line of divine order. "Binding," in the words of Dame Philosophy, "all things together in their own order" and in an "unbreakable chain of causes," it destines the love and marriage of Palamon and Emelye from two monumental wars in human history. But the beginning of this line extends back, in turn, through the vast history of Thebes and its own progressive struggle in the line of human order between "noble designs and chaos." [6] This line, we have seen, is both part and epitome of the downward movement into "corruptibility" which characterizes the order of the divine. Within the Tale, it begins with a thing that *seems* perfect and stable—the world of Theseus, under the sun, in the opening lines of the poem—and descends until that world seems to become a foul prison. But in the

[5] What may be called the "definitive" poetic presentation of these characteristics in the divine order is the *Divine Comedy*, where the influence of Boethius is as clearly discernible as in the works of Chaucer. But, again, the general set of assumptions was a commonplace of medieval thought, even though they have not, I believe, been adequately recognized by present-day scholarship. Our awareness, for example, that for the medieval Christian history moved in a "straight line"—as contrasted with the "cyclical" concept in classical thought—is usually formulated in misleading terms. For the Christian from Augustine to Dante and Chaucer, the "divine" order of history is at once cyclical *and* a straight line.

[6] Cf. Muscatine, p. 929.

divine order the prisoners are not without "ransom" because the corruption or disorder of the downward movement leads to the order of the movement up.

The dying Arcite, deprived of his humanly just rewards by the inhuman god of disorder, pronounces the mystery and vanity of this world in the eyes of human logic:

> What is this world? what asketh men to have?
> Now with his love, now in his colde
>   grave.   2778

But he at the same time renews the broken bond of human brotherhood with Palamon, and thus, in the divine chain of love, the bond between man and man. Theseus in turn, and in marked contrast to all the pomp, pride, and power which constitute his "nobility" at the beginning of the poem, pronounces his world at the end to be a "wrecched" one. But in the face of this conviction his nobility now is constituted by his acceptance of and faith in the order of the First Mover. He thus renews in the chain of love the bond between man and God. Finally, in the logic of human order, Palamon's winning Emelye seems to stand as a crowning inadequacy to all that has gone before. Yet this concluding judgment and action of the temporal lord renews in his human world not only the line of Thebes which began with Cadmus and Amphion, but also the bond of peace between Thebans and Greeks. It also renews in the divine chain of love the bond between man and woman. Thus within the narrative of the poem the upward movement of the divine order is "Convertynge al unto his propre welle/From which it is dirryved," even

though in the wisdom of the temporal lord it has all amounted to making "vertu of necessitee."

But in the more "deeply penetrating" view of the poem—which has moved from the warfare to the wedding of this temporal lord in its opening phase, and from warfare to wedding in the major portion of its narrative line—the necessity is part of a larger order. The ups and downs of Fortune with which the poem and this paper began are finally the ups and downs of the order decreed by the First Mover. And we, accordingly, can see with Chaucer—and in the words of Dame Philosophy—not only that Providence binds all things together "in their own order" but also

> Et quae motu concitat ire,
> Sistit retrahens ac uaga firmat.
> Nam nisi rectos reuocans itus
> Flexos iterum cogat in orbes,
> Quae nunc stabilis continet ordo
> Dissaepta suo fonte fatiscant.
> Hic est cunctis communis amor
> Repetuntque boni fine teneri,
> Quia non aliter durare queant,
> Nisi conuerso rursus amore
> Refluant causae quae dedit esse.   IV, m. 6

[Those things which He impels by motion to pass away He also restrains by drawing them back and making firm all that strays. For unless He were to draw together again those things which depart, and recall them into the circles of their true paths, they, now bound together by a stable order, would perish, divided from their source. This is the common bond of love, and all things ask anew to be held by the end of the good. For in no way might they endure unless, by love which has turned round again, they come back to the cause which has given them being.]

E. M. W. Tillyard

Plot-Obliquity in Chaucer's *Miller's Tale*

MY LAST EXAMPLE of plot-obliquity is Chaucer's *Miller's Tale*. This is usually thought a brilliantly-told piece of bawdry, no more: coarse fun plus one of the familiar Chaucerian features, narrative power. Actually it is a consummate piece of obliquity, yet so elusive, so apt to turn another front to you when you read it again, that to explain the obliquity is tantalisingly difficult. And yet *not* to call it oblique at once lands you in worse trouble. Of all great English poets Chaucer is the most patently sane; but if he spent his best skill of plotting and character-drawing on mere pleasant "harlotrye" he must have been temporarily mad. For it is the most brilliantly plotted of all the *Tales* and the character-sketches in no way yield to those of the Prologue. It is in the clear, economical style of Chaucer's maturity: the earlier padding or rambling have disappeared. What was he after that he should take so much trouble?

Chaucer will not tell us: although he created his own opportunity; for the Miller did not begin his tale without discussion. When the Knight had finished, the Host very reasonably asked the Monk, who of the pilgrims came next in social seniority, to have the next turn. But the Miller had grown unruly with ale and insisted on breaking in. The Host did not like to cross him and let him have his way. Chaucer interposes with his apology to the reader that the Miller *would* tell his tale and that he can take no responsibility for it:

What sholde I more seyn, but this Millere
He nolde his wordes for no man forbere,
But tolde his cherles tale in his manere;

Me thinketh that I shal reherce it here.
And therfore every gentil wight I preye,
For goddes love, demeth nat that I seye
Of evel entente, but that I moot reherce
Hir tales alle, be they bettre or werse,
Or elles falsen som of my matere.
And therfore, who-so list it nat y-here,
Turne over the leef, and chese another tale;
For he shal finde y-nowe, grete and smale,
Of storial thing that toucheth gentillesse,
And eek moralitee and holinesse;
Blameth nat me if that ye chese amis.
The Miller is a cherl, ye knowe wel this;
So was the Reve, and othere many mo,
And harlotrye they tolden bothe two.
Avyseth yow and putte me out of blame;
And eek men shal nat make ernest of
    game.   A 3186

Is this no more than Chaucer's way of telling the reader to skip the bawdry if he likes? Hardly: the specious apology of the first lines, the pretence that he had to be true to what his characters narrated (when he need not have introduced low characters at all), is only the prelude to more speciousness. "Let the squeamish reader turn the page and he will find virtuous matter enough; and don't let him blame *me* if he chooses amiss." On the surface it means no more than that if the virtuous reader choose amiss (that is, to read a bawdy tale) it is not Chaucer's fault, because other fare has been provided. But . . . *choose amiss* is ambiguous: it might mean one thing to the virtuous reader and to Chaucer another. It *could* mean, "If you're such a fool as to skip what you, if you had any taste, could see after a few lines was going to be one of my best sto-

Reprinted by permission of Chatto and Windus, London, and Macmillan, New York, from E. M. W. Tillyard, *Poetry Direct and Oblique*, revised edition, London, 1945, pp. 85–92. First published 1934.

ries, blame your own foolish and prudish self, not *me* for having thrown dust in your eyes." However, though Chaucer lets us know that he takes *The Miller's Tale* seriously, of what the seriousness is composed his prefatory lines give no hint.

Like *Little T. C.*,[1] *The Miller's Tale* gets its supreme effect by a single stroke of plot, and gives us warrant for that effect by the excellence both of subordinate plot-features and of other parts of the poem. Indeed these other features are so good that, as in *Lycidas*, it is impossible to isolate the obliquity into plot alone. We have to do with the complicated obliquity of great poetry. I shall have to go to some length to substantiate this.

The story opens with the description of Nicholas, an Oxford undergraduate, who has lodgings with John, a well-to-do but stupid carpenter. Thirty lines of Chaucer's innocent-sounding verse fix the man's character for good and show us that we are reading a careful work of art. Nicholas was a "poor scholar," but nevertheless he had an elegant room to himself (unlike most poor scholars). He looked like a girl and scented himself. His hobbies were astrology, through which he was particularly good at foretelling the weather, and music. His favorite song was *Angelus ad Virginem*, an actual Annunciation hymn: but, when we remember that with his girlish appearance he looked something like an angel himself, we suspect a further meaning in his song's title. (Throughout the poem there is a delicate mixing of the sacred and the obscene.) The last two lines of the description are the purest honey of Chaucer's irony:

And thus this swete clerk his tyme spente
After his freendes finding and his
    rente.   A 3220

In other words, this sly and idle undergraduate wastes his time with a thorough-

---

[1] Poem by Marvell, discussed earlier in *Poetry Direct and Oblique.*—Ed.

ness that fluctuates with his own income and his friends' subsidies.

The first piece of plotting is to put, without a word of comment, a short description of the carpenter alongside that of Nicholas. In twelve lines Chaucer shows us, self-doomed and star-crossed, the comic victim, elaborates his irony, and gives us the one possible hint of what the oblique features of his story may mean:

This Carpenter had wedded newe a wyf
Which that he lovede more than his lyf;
Of eightetene yeer she was of age.
Ialous he was, and heeld her narwe in cage,
For she was wilde and yong, and he was old,
And demed himself ben lyk a cokewold.
He knew nat Catoun, for his wit was rude,
That bad man sholde wedde his similitude.
Men sholde wedden after hir estaat,
For youthe and elde is often at debaat.
But sith that he was fallen in the snare,
He moste endure, as other folk, his
    care.   A 3232

To bring the carpenter and "Catoun" together is exquisitely ludicrous: and the couplet in which Chaucer does so is tight packed with implications. The gravity with which he suggests that if the carpenter had had the advantages of reading Cato he might have avoided his error is perfect comedy; and radiating from it are the ironic propositions that the working classes ought to read Cato and the like, because these are the only means of access to the mother-wit which is the common heritage of the folk, and that those who have read Cato never by any chance fall into the carpenter's error. Further, Chaucer insinuates, "I know I am a book-worm and adore theoretical wisdom, but I laugh at myself for it," and "I hope that some of my readers may not know that I am laughing at myself but may make fools of themselves by thinking themselves wiser than I am and calling me obtuse and academic." The last two lines give clearly and briefly the comic setting. They place the victim in the light of remorseless reason, but they do not isolate him from society. He is like other sinners against the wisdom of the race; not like the tragic victim, erring but mysteriously singled out by Fate for special suffering. We have to do with the way of the world, not the ways of God.

Sandwiching the carpenter ruthlessly between the "swete clerk" and her fragrant self, Alison is next described. She is a brilliant study in black and white, and her wanton eye, black as a sloe, under her plucked eyebrows, settles the elderly husband's fate more firmly than ever. Then the action begins. The carpenter has work at the Abbey of Osney, and is sometimes absent. Nicholas and Alison soon arrange to go to bed together at the first convenient opportunity. The arrangement made, "this gode wyf," Chaucer tells us, went on a saint's day to church,

Christes owne werkes for to wirche,

with her forehead shining as bright as day; and her piety introduces us to the fourth character, the flamboyant Absolon, a "parish-clerk." His curly gold hair, which stuck out like a fan, his red complexion and grey eyes, his red and blue clothes, contrast with the hard black and white in Alison's picture. And in character this merry and versatile man, who made music in all the taverns, is very different from the secretive Nicholas. There is in fact an elaborate plot-contrast between the characters. Absolon, who enjoys his duty of censing the wives, is smitten with Alison. Instead of working secretly and swiftly, he serenades her and pesters her with presents. He even plays Herod in a Miracle Play to attract her attention. Alison prefers the man on the spot.

Then follows the main intrigue. The carpenter, credulous of Nicholas's weather-wisdom, is persuaded that the stars foretell a second flood next Monday; he must hang three great kneading-troughs from the roof-beams for Alison, Nicholas, and himself, with provisions and an axe each for cut-

ting loose when the water comes. Farcical in itself, Chaucer keeps the plot to comedy by the brilliant pictures of domestic life the story unfolds: the man-servant peeping through the hole made for the cat into Nicholas's room and seeing Nicholas feigning a swoon with gaping mouth and goggle eyes; servant and master prizing open the door. Moreover the plot is tightly controlled. After the three have climbed their new-made ladders into their tubs, the stupid carpenter, just because he was dog-tired from all the work he had to do, falls into a dead sleep, which he advertises by snoring, "for his heed mislay." Nicholas and Alison climb down their ladders and proceed to make the best use of their opportunity.

But there had been another consequence of the main intrigue. The carpenter had stayed away from his work at Osney. Now Absolon, happening to be at this place on the Monday, makes discreet inquiries about the carpenter. He is told that perhaps the carpenter is away for a couple of days buying wood. Absolon thinks that now is his chance; and in the small hours of the morning begins serenading outside the window of the room where Nicholas and Alison are in bed together. Alison tells him to go away, but he persists, and our whole attention is then fixed on the ensuing farce: the carpenter snores remote from our attention. Absolon begs at least a kiss, and is granted one, but not of the kind he expected. Vowing revenge, and cured for good of his amorous imaginings, he borrows a hot iron from the blacksmith and returns for another kiss. This time Nicholas comes to the window, to get the hot iron clapped to his buttocks. And then the miracle happens, and the different pieces of the plot fly together; for Nicholas in his pain yells for water, the carpenter starts out of his sleep, hears the cry, thinks the Flood has come, and cutting the rope, crashes down on the floor beneath. The surprise, the sudden union of the two themes, is sublime. It is as if, for a fraction of a second, the heavens opened and we saw all the gods watching the trivial and ridiculous human comedy below.

The Miller's Tale is a coarse story. But though Chaucer enjoyed the coarseness, he made it strictly subserve the main ends of the plot; for it is the very outrageousness of the farce which, drawing the reader's mind away from the main plot, leaves it at the poet's disposal when he chooses to recall it.

Chaucer ends with the mathematical morality proper to comedy: the characters get what they have deserved:

> Thus swyved was the carpenteres wyf,
> For al his keping and his ialousye;
> And Absolon hath kist hir nether ye;
> And Nicholas is scalded in the toute!
> This tale is doon, and god save al the
>   route!   A 3854

What of Alison? Nothing is said of her reward, nor need it be. She had fulfilled her part of the equation beforehand by the anticipatory punishment of being married to a jealous old husband.

I have mentioned the main features of the poem: the great stroke of surprise through the plot, the exact, almost mathematical working out of the plot generally, the unerring characterisation, and the closeness to actual life. Taken together, what do they mean? Mathematical perfection of plot need mean very little. In that kind of perfection (apart from Chaucer's stroke of surprise) a play of Somerset Maugham is as well contrived as *The Miller's Tale:* yet it is hollow; the plot means little more than a high ingenuity. But in conjunction with the characterisation Chaucer's brilliant plot means a great deal. Comedy deals with individual caprice at variance with society; and society, implying a norm and limitations, must win in the end. These limitations can be expressed in more than one way. Restoration Comedy expresses them by the code of manners implied by what the characters say. Chaucer too expresses them, but far more obliquely, through the perfect orderliness of his plot, and also by the elegant economy of his language. Against this order his charming but offending victims are set, and they get their reward. Not that he judges them morally, but he shows them up against the normal background of what the world insists on being. Chaucer's extreme sensitiveness and sympathy extend the comic view of life to a very unusual range.

But the meaning of *The Miller's Tale* goes beyond the normally comic. How much significance the plot yields depends largely on how seriously the features other than plot are to be taken. Now Chaucer's characterisation should be taken very seriously indeed. However direct in appearance, it has an oblique meaning, and however objective, it has a psychological correlative in Chaucer's mind. The quality it most expresses is a strong, acute, and eager sensibility. Chaucer absorbed and was absorbed by the characters of those around him with vehemence: the kind of vehemence Keats showed towards pure sensation and D. H. Lawrence towards his birds, beasts, and flowers. Supplemented by the sensibility, vouched for, as it were, by it, the plot of *The Miller's Tale* acquires an abstract significance analogous to that of good music or of the best Byzantine mosaics. And when Chaucer delivers his master-stroke, bringing back the carpenter into the story through Nicholas's yelling for water, he gets beyond the social bounds of comedy and impels the reader's mind to exult and to expand as it does in enjoying the very greatest art. From the side of comedy Chaucer loses himself in an *O Altitudo;* and feelings akin to those of religious wonder are the ultimate obliquity issuing from all the parts and especially from the plot of *The Miller's Tale*.

Raymond Preston

Tales of the Man of Law and Clerk

SOME READERS have found the Man of Law's prologue oddly contrived, though passages in the same strain occur on the slightest provocation in the *Romance of the Rose*—and the speech of the Man of Law could hardly be more appropriate to his description in the *Prologue:*

> Discreet he was and of greet reverence—
> He semed swich, his wordes weren so
>   wise.   A 313

The rich justice delivers himself "like a Pope" on the advantages of being at least a rich merchant, such as the merchant from whom he heard the tale; and with rich merchants it begins. Not only did Chaucer apparently translate the ascetic treatise *De Contemptu Mundi* of Innocent III, for the good of his soul or of the souls of others; he also successfully incorporated in the *Tale of the Man of Law* itself extracts like those which answer the drunkenness of the Miller and the lust of the churls' tales. Here, in fact, is a *legende and a lyf*, as the Miller tipsily foretold.

Yet it is self-sufficient; there is in any case no certain connexion in the manuscripts between this tale and another; and so I shall pause for a moment to anticipate the similar story of the Clerk's. That is also about a spiritual principle, and about the struggles of a soul to abide by it. As Professor Raleigh once said, Griselde of the *Clerk's Tale* is not a patient woman; she is Patience. And in the same way the Man of Law's Constance is Constancy or Fortitude. The Man of Law's performance is more episodic, more various, than the Clerk's, and the episodes have richer associations of

folktale. In the *Clerk's Tale* Chaucer keeps more strictly to his theme and, incidentally, to his sources. Of this apparent restriction to the letter there is an example when the Marquis of Saluzzo prepares to wed Griselde:

> Grisilde of this, God woot, ful innocent,
> That for hire shapen was al this array,
> To fecchen water at a welle is went,
> And cometh hoom as soone as ever she may;
> For wel she hadde herd seyd that thilke day
> The markys sholde wedde; and if she myghte,
> She wolde fayn han seyn som of that
>   sighte.   E 280

I see no hint in these lines of the interesting possibilities suggested by Professor Manly, who proposed that the same well in the primitive version was an entrance to the other world, a Well at the World's End. If the carrying of water bears significance beyond Griselde's peasant life, it has biblical associations of a kind certainly present elsewhere:

> But hye God somtyme sende kan
> His grace into a litel oxes stalle. . . .   E 207

> The markys cam, and gan hire for to calle;
> And she set doun hir water pot anon,
> Biside the thresshfold, in an oxes
>   stalle.[1] . . .   E 291

So far as we know, Chaucer could not have found a stable either in his Petrarch or in *Le Livre Griseldis*.

[1] For the *oxes stalle*, the French text printed by Professor Severs has only *un petit hoste et mainnaige*, and the Latin *pauperum tuguria* (*Sources and Analogues*, pp. 302–3).

Reprinted by permission from Raymond Preston, *Chaucer*, London and New York, Sheed and Ward, 1952, pp. 201–205, 250–256, 305–309.

The tale of Griselde contains very few verses which have power to fix themselves in the memory; the narrative is never to that extent at high tension. Yet it accumulates an emotion which is very impressive indeed. One can test this, to one's own satisfaction, by marking certain lines that stand out as they come in the story, and then reading those lines alone some time later. Re-read in this way, they do not give the quality of the whole poem, they do not recall the development to a climax; they refuse to be samples. We have often been told that it is not possible, or at least not fair, to quote from Chaucer. But it is certainly possible, and more than fair, to quote from the *Tale of the Man of Law*. What we recollect of it is not the pattern, still less the details, of the story; but a range of the highest points of the verse. Everyone who has read this tale with some attention to its poetry will have been held by the lines which describe, through remembered glimpses of a condemned man in the crowd, the helplessness of Constance at her trial. They have just a hint of that contrary stanza of the *Troilus* in which he who was to die is suddenly rescued, and finds himself in the arms of his lady.

> Have ye nat seyn somtyme a pale face
> Among a prees, of hym that hath be lad
> Toward his deeth, wher as hym gat no grace
> And swich a colour in his face hath had
> Men myghte knowe his face that was bistad
> Amonges alle the faces in that route?
> So stant Custance, and looketh hire
>   aboute.[2]   B 651

The repetition of a single word conveys appearance and re-appearance of the pallor of the man as he is led to execution. It is a remarkable expression of terror, and probably the most fitting and frequent quotation from Chaucer in our period of World War. But Chaucer was not greatly interested in the expression of terror, or in any intensity which might upset the equilibrium of the intelligence. For once he would show

[2] Compare *Troilus and Criseyde* III, 1240–6.

that he could produce a good line in melodrama, even a sequence and a "cut" that would satisfy a twentieth-century amateur of the cinema. And in the whole tale Chaucer was doing, on a higher level, what a good film director tries to do with commonplace material; for, however fine the remote origins of the story may be, Trivet's telling is undistinguished; and Chaucer added to it some of his best exhibition verses. Such are (a flower of evil) the close of the speech of the *sowdanesse,* and the farewell of Constance to her father—above all, her address to the Cross.

> "O cleere, o welful auter, hooly croys,
> Red of the Lambes blood ful of pitee,
> That wessh the world fro the olde iniquitee,
> Me fro the feend and fro his clawes kepe,
> That day that I shal drenchen in the depe.
>
> Victorious tree, proteccioun of trewe,
> That oonly worthy were for to bere
> The Kyng of Hevene with his woundes newe,
> The white Lamb, that hurt was with the spere,
> Flemere of feendes out of hym and here
> On which thy lymes feithfully extenden,
> Me kepe, and yif me myght my lyf
>   t'amenden."   B 462

This is the clarity of the medieval religious vision; the Chaucerian *cleere* is hardly translatable in modern English. This is a fulfilment of the promise of his version of Guillaume de Deguilleville praising the Virgin. At the ninth line the verse is incandescent. Constance echoes the liturgy; and throughout the story—even through its crudities of plot—she in some way represents the Church Militant. The tale is told with an excess of rhetorical skill that might be expected from a lawyer who has been raised to the poetic stage of a Chaucerian pilgrimage: otherwise it no more appears to fit its narrator than the story of Appius and Virginia appears to fit the Physician.[3]

[3] Paul F. Beichner, *Speculum* January 1948, observes in B 204–31 a knowledge of canon law; but a poet wishing to dramatize a character can draw on more than information.

Both the *Clerk's Tale* and the *Tale of the Man of Law* may be seen, I think, as a medieval prognostic of Shakespeare's later plays. If we allow for the fact that Shakespeare was writing for the theatre, composing verse which had to make its effect in action, it is not so very difficult to associate Constance and Imogen, to compare the closing scenes of *Pericles* and the *Winter's Tale* with the reconciliation of Walter and Griselde, or the recognition of Maurice. That which was lost, we say at the end, is now found: and I do not know another writer who has given so much of the joy of the finding. Chaucer set it down; Shakespeare orchestrated it.

* * * * * * * * *

Now I should like to look a little more closely at Chaucer's *poetics,* and to propose a fresh interpretation of his poem. For I believe that the *Clerk's Tale* has been underestimated, because incompletely understood.

It is as interesting to compare passages of Petrarch's Latin and the French redaction with the poetry that Chaucer made out of them, as it is to consider those lines of *Antony and Cleopatra* in which Shakespeare closely followed North's *Plutarch;* and the methods of two great poets could hardly be more unlike. Chaucer's style is so restrained, so chaste, that no quotation can convey an idea of the whole tale. The lines I shall give are not intended to represent it, and should be read in their context.

sed virilis senilisque animus virgineo latebat in pectore

Toutesfoiz courage meur et ancien estoit muciez et enclos en sa virginite

Yet in the brest of hire virginitee
Ther was enclosed rype and sad corage [4] E 220

---

[4] The Latin quotation may be translated, literally, "but the spirit of manhood and of age lay hidden in her maiden bosom"; and the French, "yet the spirit of ripeness and of old age was hidden and enclosed in her virginity."

The Latin and French extracts are taken from *Epistolae Seniles,* Book XVII, Letter III, and from

Here Chaucer could not have translated the French much more literally within his metre; but the difference is that lingering emphasis of rhyme and rhythm which makes certain words shine with clarity. The next version is only slightly less literal:

s'il n'eust sceu qu'elle amast parfaitement ses enffans, il l'eust tenue pour suspette et mauvaise femme, et eust crue celle fermeté et constance venir de couraige d'aucune crueuse voulenté

       . . . if that he
Ne hadde soothly knowen therbifoore
That parfitly hir children loved she,
He wolde have wend that of som subtiltee,
And of malice, or of cruel corage,
That she hadde suffred this with sad visage.

But wel he knew that next hymself, certayn,
She loved hir children best in every
    wyse.[5] E 695

The alteration, the prominence given to the term *subtiltee,* emphasize sinister possibilities; just as, in a larger context, Chaucer finds the persons opposed to Griselde more evil and, without any trace of overemphasis, underlines the contrasts of character.

reverenter atque humiliter

humblement et en tres grant reverence

And she set doun hir water pot anon,
Biside the thresshfold, in an oxes stalle,
And doun upon hir knees she gan to falle,
And with sad contenance kneleth stille,
Til she had herd what was the lordes
    wille.[6] E 294

This is clearly imagination of objects and acts which *mean more* than the general

---

Le Livre Griseldis respectively, in the texts given by J. B. Severs in *Sources and Analogues.* Dr. Severs has also published a study under the title *The Literary Relationships of Chaucer's Clerkes Tale* (New Haven, 1942).

[5] The French reads "if he had not known that she perfectly loved her children, he would have held her a suspicious and evil woman, and have believed this steadiness and constancy to come from some cruel will."

[6] The Latin has only "reverently and humbly"; the French, "humbly and with very great reverence."

phrasing of the prose. Through a long tradition of folktale Psyche has become, in these
lines, the maid for whom her lord prepared a marriage-feast, the maid recalling
the Virgin, recalling Christ, in humility and
suffering; but obedient, in the first place,
to a power which is not divine. The power
is to be—though how should Griselde
know?—a cruelty in itself wholly unjusti-
fied, yet in the event proving, through divine grace,[7] the strength of a single virtue.
We may set down this Oxenford logic: that
a single virtue is an abstraction, but Griselde personifies a single virtue, therefore
Griselde is an unnatural mother. Yet if
there is one line that we can quote to suggest the poetic quality of the *Clerk's Tale*,
it is

O tendre, o deere, o yonge children myne . . .
                                        E 1093

Chaucer, against the laws of probability,
has given Griselde the essence of the human
feeling. That is how a mother would speak
if she could speak poetry. A single virtue is
difficult, true; grant the possibility, and the
virtue of Griselde appears inexhaustible.

What I have so far said is about less than
half of the *Clerk's Tale:* it is to show the
poetry of the persuasiveness of the Clerk,
which is a kind of dramatic poetry. In terms
of the liberal arts, with which the narrator
was familiar, the tale is a superb piece of
Rhetoric and Music; but its Dialectic is
quite untenable, as Petrarch himself, and
Chaucer's Clerk, were aware.

This story it has seemed good to me to weave
anew, in another tongue, not so much that it might
stir the matrons of our times to imitate the patience of this wife—who seems to me scarcely
imitable—as that it might stir all those who read
it to imitate the woman's steadfastness, at least;
so that they may have the resolution to perform
for God what this woman performed for her husband. For He cannot be tempted with evil, as saith
James the Apostle, and He himself tempts no man.
Nevertheless, He often proves us and suffers us to

be vexed with many a grievous scourge; not that
He may know our spirit, for that He knew ere we
were made, but that our own frailty may be made
known to us through notable private signs.

This storie is seyd, nat for that wyves sholde
Folwen Grisilde as in humylitee,
For it were importable, though they wolde;
But for that every wight, in his degree,
Sholde be constant in adversitee
As was Grisilde; therfore Petrak writeth
This storie, which with heigh stile he enditeth.

For, sith a womman was so pacient
Unto a mortal man, wel moore us oghte
Receyven al in gree that God us sent;
For greet skile is, he preeve that he wroghte.
But he ne tempteth no man that he boghte,
As seith Seint Jame, if ye his pistel rede;
He preveth folk al day, it is no drede,

And suffreth us, as for oure exercise,
With sharpe scourges of adversitee
Ful ofte to be bete in sondry wise;
Nat for to knowe oure wyl; for certes he,
Er we were born, knew al oure freletee;
And for oure beste is al his governaunce.
Lat us thanne lyve in vertuous
    suffraunce.[8]   E 1162

Only if the husband represents a supernatural power, as in the earliest versions
of the tale, is Griselde's behaviour logically
justified. The Wife of Bath had enough
sense not to make a god of a husband, and
was quite capable of perceiving the fallacy
of Griselde's submission to Walter as to a
creator of life who has the right to destroy.
She was also capable of recognizing, at
least for argument's sake, what was to be
admired in such humility. Both Alice and
the Clerk, whatever their intentions, have
shown the evil of domination in marriage,
and the *ernestful matere* of the *Clerk's Tale*,
in the end, is high comedy. . . .

In composing the Clerk's *Envoy* Chaucer
may have remembered again the simpler

---

[7] E 395: *God hath swich favour sent hire of his
grace. . . .*

[8] I have quoted from R. D. French's translation
of Petrarch's Latin. The original is given as a
marginal gloss in several MSS.: see *The Text of
the Canterbury Tales* ed. Manly and Rickert III,
pp. 507–8.

ridicule of Jean de Meun: the jealous husband telling of Penelope and Lucretia, and observing that such women were nowhere to be found.[9] The master of logic coming forward with his song in honour of the Wife of Bath is one of the most amusing spectacles on pilgrimage; and it is an affront to a great comedian of Christendom to ask whether Chaucer really intended his *envoy* for the Clerk. The scribe's heading is not to be taken.

Thus Chaucer presents his "drama": less *in* verse than *through* verse, so that we can look beyond the immediate persuasion, and the emotion of the moment. I do not say that he is writing poetry for us to "see through"—that would be too obvious to suit the Oxford scholar. The simple feeling is there, of reverence for Griselde; unblurred; but complicated without confusion, to a degree which may place the modern reader, for a time, out of his depth. The poetry is not cancelled by the comedy,

and the comic *envoy* is no less poetic than the tale. And when I consider the poetry I am reminded that Wordsworth was a reader of Chaucer, and indeed was almost forestalled by the calmness of the Clerk. For Wordsworth's finest work is essentially a firm desire for the single quality that is already there, in a large and various relation to many very different qualities, in Chaucer; the quality of *still rootedness*.

And richely his doghter maryed he
Unto a lord, oon of the worthieste
Of al Ytaille; and than in pees and reste
His wyves fader in his court he kepeth,
Til that the soule out of his body
    crepeth.[10]   E 1134

The great technicians of art—among whom are Chaucer, and the composer Guillaume de Machaut, and Bach—assimilate, discover, re-discover so much that they seem to anticipate later developments almost casually. . . .

Epilogue

I TAKE a last glance, before the 550th anniversary of his passing, at Chaucer in that time, and in this: not for a summary but a fresh look at the same view, which has a slightly different light every time we really regard it. Turn towards the later fourteenth century, and you see building of smooth surface but extraordinary complication, and a delta of thought that is equally intricate. The initiative both in the architecture and in the philosophy of Europe had passed to England. It was an era of critical intelligence and vitality of invention. And in spite of all its evils, it had not yet lost the theological virtues. Then the intellect hardens; stone solidifies. In verse, all but the anonymous lose a sense of movement, and Lydgate suffers from muscular rheumatism. Skelton's brilliant and desperate entertainment is a final flicker of the tail of medieval England. And Shakespeare, looking back

to the reign of Henry IV, saw not so very much more of fraud or riot or opportunism than was visible to Chaucer, but a spiritual disease of a whole people. All things are possible except to despair.

But return to the architecture, in which the continuity of the middle ages will be here and now as long as our cathedrals remain. Chaucer still saw himself within an order of Catholic Europe, in a Europe broken and divided, an England diseased and heretical. "To lead the things which are lower to the things which are higher through the things which are intermedi-

9 *Le Roman de la Rose* ed. Langlois, 8608ff.

10 I refer particularly to the last line, which is not taken from the Latin or French source. The same metaphor occurs in E 121: *In crepeth age alwey, as stille as stoon.* . . . Compare Wordsworth's *Evening Walk* 354, *The Old Cumberland Beggar* 59–61, *The Excursion* VII, 707–9. Dr. D. J. Enright draws my attention also to a likeness between Griselda and the Wordsworthian maiden.

ate": that is the great principle of Catholic order: which needs more than a few generations of division or disease or heresy to destroy it. Chaucer was no regressive, but a most conscious mind of his age: opposing to disorder not the tense, single-minded elevation of High Gothic, of the *Divine Comedy*, but the Decorated of his own humour, that is a humour of England and of Europe as well. In an exact sense he is a more philosophical poet than Dante, though Matthew Arnold was right to imply that if we had to lose the one or the other we had better hold on to Dante. Chaucer was constantly aware of the problems of evil and of the freedom of human will; he knew the work of philosophers, and without being a philosopher himself, had the philosophical habit of mind, the capacity to delay conclusion. Perhaps this is one reason why he left so much incomplete. But the Gothic builder was always telling his stories, and what remained unfinished was not therefore fragmentary, for it was never within a closed system. Nor are the *Canterbury Tales*. And for the patterns of these "fragments" there is analogy in other arts: the medieval motet in which praise of the pious clergy, and satire of the hypocritical, could both be sung together with a scriptural text in musical counterpoint: or the beautiful early fourteenth-century decoration of Queen Mary's Psalter, in which a religious set-piece shares a page with an informal hawking party.

There is more to be said about the philosophers, and much more than I can say here. The reader of fourteenth-century English literature has too much of the superficies of social history forced upon his attention by commentators, and too little of the history of ideas. He turns away from the faggots and hides and pitchers, wanting a "background" of the kind that Professor Basil Willey has assembled for later times. Chaucer lived in an age that had been enlightened by St. Thomas Aquinas: who described man not merely as a spirit imprisoned in flesh, but as a compositum of

body and soul. Now the *logical probability* of the Resurrection of the Body, as well as the revelation, is a doctrine one would almost be inclined to invent for our poet, if it were not already so authoritatively behind him. Sense-experience, taught Aquinas, was to be respected; for through it we could attain, by analogy, to a concept of the infinite First Cause. *Nihil in intellectu quod prius non fuerit in sensu.* The greatest thinker of the past several centuries allowed an intelligent man to be in some sense at home in the world, so long as he was not too preoccupied with it. Thus, in the end, Troilus laughs, and the Parson has his turn. Chaucer was at ease with the balanced minds. He sensed the futility of medieval logic in decline, and, referring to Bradwardine, surely knew also of the Augustinian reaction against unfruitful argument in his day. He understood so much of complexity in human nature, and of our place in the universe, that we can see him a respected comedian in company with the best scholastics. And scholasticism can introduce us, in a new way, to comedy. Let us attend, for instance, to the developing thought of Aquinas and, later, of Scotus the Subtle Doctor, on the problem of individuation. What we at first appreciate in Chaucer's pilgrims is what Scotus would call the *haecceitas* of each particular person, which is a notion very much newer to the fourteenth century than to us, who have suffered from exaggerating the separate reality of the individual. What we do not readily understand in Chaucer is the *generalizing* power which Blake so finely admired. We could too easily pursue a parallel, once it is pointed out, between the critical development of fourteenth-century thought and the development of Chaucer's own work. When Durandus of Saint-Pourçain replied to the problem of individuation by saying that the individual is given in experience, and that knowledge of particulars is a higher knowledge than the abstract; and when in William of Ockham the knower comes face to face with the known without the Thomist apparatus of knowing in between—something is happening that is related to an abandonment of allegory in literature. But fortunately the old ways are not suddenly forgotten, even when they are changed; and our comedian remains in charity with the angelic doctor.[11] However receptive, he was unshaken by the dangerous tendencies of science or psychology, to which I shall return in a moment. If we eliminate the senses in which all of his work was not religious, there remains a sense in which it is. It could afford, in spite of "everything," to take immense reserves of conviction, of assurance, for granted. It could occur only in a certain civilization, when that civilization had reached its highest point—and the higher the civilization, the steeper the downward gradient that the civilized think they can stand. So the historian might say, and not without reason; but forgetting that Chaucer is still alive in the mind, and still (Arnold was just again) central. Call this the epitaph of Cambiuskan, but Chaucer's true testimonial: *of his corage as any centre stable.* Chaucer surveyed the world from a centre apparently different from that to which Dante penetrated through and beyond the world; but the centre is the same, of the sphere that Aquinas describes, whose centre is everywhere and circumference nowhere intelligible; and Dante was permitted to see the whole sphere. In another way Chaucer is central. His mind was at the centre of his humility; and humility, agree Walter Hilton and T. S. Eliot, is endless. In a third way Chaucer is central, between the extremes of life and character which he balanced for comedy. And we have to struggle to the centre he could always find.

Chaucer is living, but we cannot get back to Chaucer. In comparison with America, Lord Russell has assured us, Europe has not entirely lost the medieval tradition; and that may be why scholars inquire more actively in America than in England about the greatest medieval English poet. The belief in the force of human will and energy, which was sown a little before his time, has left him uncorrupted. We should not speak of "Chaucer's world," for Chaucer is the poet of men humble and happy in God's world. And a study of the changes of fortune of the word *will* can be very improving. It has now degenerated, except in technical usage, to the sense of *drive*—the power that keeps a nose to the grindstone or a nation behind a leader. The violence of modern science, and cinema, is its disease: the present weakness of will. In the fourteenth century it still meant the power of choosing, loving, resting in, the good: and Chaucer's is the last great poetry that accepts this medieval peace. Villon leaves his testament, and the next event is a war of separate wills on the renaissance stage. Later English literature is either comparatively limited in vision, or Manichean in tendency. That is to say, it is inclined either to ignore or to dramatize the black and evil god; and when it dramatizes, to be closer to an over-excited reading of the *Parson's Tale* than to Chaucer. Nobody in his senses will go back five hundred and fifty years as to a golden age, or insist that Shakespeare arrived too late. Shakespeare stands: the middle age had its poet of intensity in Dante. And in Dante the separate human will is subsumed in an endless sounding of *terza rima.* Chaucer is our medieval poet of serenity, a poet *qui fait rire dans l'âme,* and the only one of his stature, I suspect, in whom contentment is not an enemy of genius. I doubt whether anyone has come so near to disproving the

[11] There is, as I have said, no *Fourteenth-Century Background;* but two recent English publications, with bibliographies, introduce the professional thinkers of the period. These are *A Sketch of Medieval Philosophy* by D. J. B. Hawkins (Sheed and Ward, 1946), and *A Short History of Western Philosophy in the Middle Ages* by S. J. Curtis (Macdonald, 1950). Frederick Copleston's *History of Philosophy* Volume II (Burns Oates, 1950) is a fuller survey from Augustine to Scotus, and Volume III will begin with Ockham and the fourteenth century.

view that no major work of art can be produced without the aid of the devil: for to him the devil is finally impotent, and there remain the *clere sterres*.

But the great ironist is too present to allow me to close on a large and distant sentence. Refinement of irony, in the end, depends upon a tone of the voice: and it is a curious fact, or else a very persuasive illusion, that after these five and a half centuries one can hear the tones of certain passages of his poetry as clearly as the tones of the most recent verse in the language. However subtle or complicated medieval art becomes, it is always near to the tongue or the hand or the eye. When we try to get back to original pronunciations of poetry, Shakespeare seems to me to suffer slight pain, as if stored too long in a damp barn; but Chaucer always smiles more. And Chaucer alighting today in London would probably be amused to recognize, in so much that is unrecognizable, a certain vowel sound in Cockney. This is the man who did something for English that Dante did for Italian; the man with the most *art* of any English poet, and the easiest naturalness. So the best "introduction" to Chaucer is to listen to him, to the English he wrote.

Now preye I to hem alle that herkne this litel tretys or rede, that if there be anything in it that liketh hem, that therof they thanken our Lord Jesu Christ, of whom procedeth al wit and al goodnesse. And if ther be any thyng that displese hem, I preye hem also that they arrette it to the defaut of my unconnynge, and nat to my wil, that wolde ful fayne have seyd bettre if I hadde had connynge . . .

Charles Muscatine

The Mixed Style

The Canterbury Tales as a whole is an example of the mixed style. Each of the tales, by analogy and by contrast, takes meaning from others. The effect of the larger form, a structure of juxtapositions and tensions, is to place and control the attitudes evoked separately by its parts, to reveal their virtues and limitations in context. Some of this manipulation of attitudes is announced dramatically by rivalries among the pilgrims. The Miller and Reeve, the Summoner and Friar, are at overt personal debate. The Clerk recognizes in his envoy a relationship to the Wife of Bath. The Cook promises a comment on an innkeeper. These dramatic relationships are in turn supported, and nondramatic ones are established mutely but no less powerfully, by the choice and disposition of the literary materials themselves. Thus the Miller's dramatic announcement of

> "a noble tale for the nones
> With which I wol now quite the Knyghtes
>   tale,"   A 3127

is underscored in his tale by a resemblance to the Knight's in plot and in character grouping. The Reeve's rivalry with the Miller has similar literary support. The Host's implied comparison of the Nun's Priest with the Monk is followed by the Priest's recitation of a "tragedy" which comments on the Monk's collection of tragedies. "Criticism has detected (or suspected) a whole web of such relationships among the tales, in genre, subject, plot, characterization, and so on."

It is hard to know where to draw the line between art and algebra in these correspondences. The work is so great as to begin to generate its own relationships. Does the description of the clerk Nicholas in the *Miller's Tale*, with its verbal reminiscences of the Clerk's portrait in the *General Prologue*, announce a comparative study of clerkships? Is Chaucer's Clerk to be compared to the Wife of Bath's fifth husband? Is there a "Marriage Group"? Had Chaucer extended his poem, would the Merchant or the Monk have replied to the *Shipman's Tale?* There are provocative resemblances between the *Miller's Tale* and the *Merchant's:* do they support a philosophical comparison? One could not begin to describe the relational possibilities suggested by Chaucer's language, by phrases repeated —"pitee renneth soone in gentil herte," "allone, withouten any compaignye," [1]— and by such repeated figures as the rhetorical *comparatio* on the death of Priam, which is used to describe both Constance's departure from Rome and Chauntecleer's abduction from a chicken yard.[2] We need not pause to evaluate all these possibilities. Even what is announced in the gross stylistics of the *Canterbury Tales* shows Chaucer's tireless capacity for definition and comparison. He has a passion for relationships, and the over-all structure of the work, the linear sequence of discrete stories in various styles, meets this passion perfectly.

[1] See, respectively, *KnT* 1761, *MerchT* 1986, *SqT* 479 (cf. *LGW* F 503) ; and *KnT* 2779, *MillT* 3204.
[2] *MLT* 288–94; *NPT* B 4545–51.

Reprinted by permission of author and publisher from Charles Muscatine, *Chaucer and the French Tradition*, Berkeley and Los Angeles, University of California Press, 1957, pp. 222–223, 237–247.

We are not surprised to find something of the same structure within the individual tales. Many of them can richly stand alone as containing significant measurement within themselves. The dominant attitudes they convey are habitually conjoined with other attitudes, idiosyncrasies with norms, norms with idiosyncrasies or other norms. The perspective is created variously; it is inserted, appended, implied, disguised, or worked plainly into the main pattern of the story. Sometimes it is a matter of plot and circumstance, the irony of a wrong turning that exposes an ignorance and prepares for a defeat. Often it comes with an internal shift of style.

Virtually all the *Canterbury Tales* have some mixture of styles. The poems of dominantly religious inspiration have a realism which, if the poem is successful, as I think the *Prioress' Tale* is, melts symbolically into the conventional frame without conflict or irony. This peaceful stylistic mixture has some of the quality of the religious paradox itself; naturalism and the supernatural make peace in miracle. But in other poems the shifting style brings in whole shifts of assumptions. In poems where one style is heavily dominant, the mixture is enough to comment on, but not enough to rival the dominant attitude; thus the touches of commonsensical humor in the *Knight's Tale*, the scrap of lyricism in the *Reeve's Tale*, and the formal rhetoric in the *Canon's Yeoman's Tale* are relatively minor in effect. The *Wife of Bath's Prologue* swallows up a great mass of learned doctrine without losing its dominantly naturalistic shape. But there are a number of tales in which, as in the *Parliament of Fowls* and the *Troilus*, the mixed style is on display and becomes part of the subject of the poem. These are the tales which seem most "Chaucerian," comprehending in small space, as they do, so much of Chaucer's range.

The *Nun's Priest's Tale*

THE *Nun's Priest's Tale*, much like the *House of Fame*, turns over a world of material, yet leaves an impression that is more of an inherent quality than of a specific teaching. It is above all brilliant, varied, a virtuoso performance. Though it contains a nugget of fable morality, its theme, like that of the earlier poem, is not found in the usual places, or expressed in the usual terms. The difference from the *House of Fame*—to pass over many resemblances, as between the Eagle and the Cock—is that here a theme so much more patently exists. Though the poem is as complex as the other, it is not confused. Formerly the poet scrambled among his materials; here he sees through them. So the *Nun's Priest's Tale* not only epitomizes the *Canterbury Tales*, it fittingly serves to cap all of Chaucer's poetry. And so I put it last.

It is fitting, too, that a poetry so much involved with the French tradition should base its most representative poem on the *Roman de Renart*. I have no sympathy with the theories of common, primitive sources and isolated versions. Chaucer's "source" for the mock-heroic development of the tale can have been nothing less than the *Roman* itself. No separate animal fable or collection of fables could have presented the tale of the Cock and the Fox to him in an aura at once so cosmic and so comic. The *Manciple's Tale* is a creditable example of what Chaucer might do with an isolated moral fable. The *Nun's Priest's Tale* is greatly more expansive than fable because the *Renart* is supremely so. The Nun's Priest's disrespect is equaled in breadth only by that of his equally unbeneficed French brothers, and it is secretly defended like theirs (as I guess) by an equal acceptance of the fundamental articles of faith. The humor of the *Nun's Priest's Tale* does not come at all as near to singeing its subjects; but this is the difference between the skirmishes preceding the war and the festive fireworks commemorating it in peace.

The tale will betray with laughter any too-solemn scrutiny of its naked argument. If it is true that Chauntecleer and Pertelote are rounded characters, it is also true that they are chickens. To ask which one of them has the better in their scholarly debate over dreams is to be too solemn; it is to assume that chickens, too, are concerned with scholarship. The serious point is more in the anomalous fact of the chicken debate itself than in its outcome. The tale has recently been welcomed into the Marriage Group, but it says little about marriage that it does not unsay. With what marriage, indeed, can it be said to deal? The marriage of Chauntecleer in the varying lights of the poem is courtly and bourgeois, monogamous and polygamous, incestuous, and unsolemnized, a relationship of paramours. The tale seems to have an irreducible core of antifeminism, but by similar tokens it is feminist too:

> But sovereynly dame Pertelote shrighte,
> Ful louder than dide Hasdrubales wyf,
> Whan that hir housbonde hadde lost his lyf,
> And that the Romayns hadde brend Cartage.
> She was so ful of torment and of rage
> That wilfully into the fyr she sterte,
> And brende hirselven with a stedefast
> herte.   B 4558

The most deliciously ambiguous line in Chaucer is the Nun's Priest's "I kan noon harm of no womman divyne" (B 4456). Even the theme of Pride, which comes closer to the mark, is confounded finally by the tone of the poem:

> Bifel that Chauntecleer in al his pryde,
> His sevene wyves walkynge by his
> syde. . . .   B 4382

The difference between this and animal fable is that this cannot long be taken more seriously in one direction than in the other. Fable respects the boundary between animal fiction and the human truth it illustrates. But the whole spirit of this poem is to erase or at least to overleap the boundaries: animal and human, fiction and truth severally join and separate, change partners and flirt here. The one constancy in the poem is this shifting of focus, the Chaucerian multiple perspective which itself virtually constitutes the theme.

With the *Parliament*, the *Troilus*, and many of the *Tales* behind us, there is no difficulty in recognizing the deliberate and controlled art with which Chaucer manipulates his materials. In the *House of Fame* the transformation of Dante's golden Eagle into a loquacious pedant, the sequence of Dantean rhetoric and colloquial dialogue, leaves one in doubt between irony and inconsistency, art and chance. The superior clarity of the *Nun's Priest's Tale* at such points is owing to a more sensitive knowledge of the potency of the materials, a surer sense of their meanings in combination, and so a bolder hand in their management. The rhetoric of the Nun's Priest, like the Merchant's and the Pardoner's, is boldly rhetorical, artistically overdone. Chauntecleer's scholarship is overwhelmingly, deliciously pedantic. The opening description of the poor widow and her farm is notably compact and pointed in meaning. Its careful impression of temperance and simple sufficiency, its husbanding of sensory effect, evokes an archetypal humility. The cock's magnificence breaks out amid this carefully restrained setting with the best Chaucerian effect: it expands, climbs, brightens, then bursts like a rocket into a shower of color.

> A yeerd she hadde, enclosed al aboute
> With stikkes, and a drye dych withoute,
> In which she hadde a cok, hight Chauntecleer.
> In al the land of crowyng nas his peer.
> His voys was murier than the murie orgon
> On messe-dayes that in the chirche gon.
> Wel sikerer was his crowyng in his logge
> Than is a clokke or an abbey orlogge.
> By nature he knew ech ascencioun
> Of the equynoxial in thilke toun;
> For whan degrees fiftene weren ascended,

Thanne crew he, that it myghte nat been
  amended.
His coomb was redder than the fyn coral,
And batailled as it were a castel wal;
His byle was blak, and as the jeet it shoon;
Lyk asure were his legges and his toon;
His nayles whitter than the lylye flour,
And lyk the burned gold was his
  colour.   B 4054

The transition from rhetoric and heroics back to the naturalism of the farm has the same candid shock effect; it is, indeed, much the same shift of perspective as when the squabble in the *Parliament* interrupts the gentle pleadings of noble lovers:

O woful hennes, right so criden ye,
As, when that Nero brende the citee
Of Rome, cryden senatoures wyves
For that hir husbondes losten alle hir lyves;
Withouten gilt this Nero hath hem slayn.
Now wole I turne to my tale agayn.
This sely wydwe and eek hir doghtres two
Herden thise hennes crie and maken wo,
And out at dores stirten they anon,
And syen the fox toward the grove gon,
And bar upon his bak the cok away,
And cryden, "Out! harrow! and weylaway!
Ha! ha! the fox!" and after hym they ran,
And eek with staves many another man.
Ran Colle oure dogge, and Talbot, and
  Gerland,
And Malkyn, with a dystaf in hir hand;
Ran cow and calf, and eek the verray hogges,
So fered for the berkyng of the dogges
And shoutyng of the men and wommen eeke,
They ronne so hem thoughte hir herte
  breeke.   B 4578

Not all the stylistic transitions have so thunderous an effect, nor are the various subjects that in turn occupy the field given equal elaboration. Exemplum and authority take almost two hundred verses in the debate between cock and hen; beauty is tested in a single image:

"Madame Pertelote, so have I blis,
Of o thyng God hath sent me large grace;
For whan I se the beautee of youre face,
Ye been so scarlet reed aboute youre yen,
It maketh al my drede for to dyen."   B 4352

The complicated optics of the poem can hold a number of views simultaneously; or it can shift from one to the next and back with lightness and rapidity:

Wommennes conseils been ful ofte colde;
Wommannes conseil broghte us first to wo,
And made Adam fro Paradys to go,
Ther as he was ful myrie and wel at ese.
But for I noot to whom it myght displese,
If I conseil of wommen wolde blame,
Passe over, for I seyde it in my game.
Rede auctours, where they trete of swich
  mateere,
And what they seyn of wommen ye may heere.
Thise been the cokkes wordes, and nat myne;
I kan noon harm of no womman divyne. B 4456

It can produce a continuous band of overlapping views, as when Chauntecleer's magnificence passes into courtly love, and thence by the way of dreams and medical science into a most unromantic, domestic familiarity: "For Goddes love, as taak som laxatyf" (B 4133). Whatever the mode of altering and manipulating perspective, however, the fact of manipulation is always clear.

The context that confirms each particular stylistic device in its mock heroics is very broad. The plot of the poem, the description of the narrator, the dramatics of the pilgrimage frame, and the very sequence of the tales here all contribute to the one process of multiplying contradictions. The rich, jolly, secular Monk, with the fine horse and clinking bridle bells, will relate nothing but a series of tragedies:

Tragedie is to seyn a certeyn storie,
As olde bookes maken us memorie,
Of hym that stood in greet prosperitee,
And is yfallen out of heigh degree
Into myserie, and endeth wrecchedly.   B 3167

The Nun's Priest, whose "foul and lene" horse bespeaks a poverty much fitter for gloom and whose anonymity prepares us for nothing more, tells a superbly humane tale, perhaps the best of all. The plot is tragic, until it ends happily. It is an allegory of the Fall—leaving Man, somewhat wiser, still in possession of his paradise, or his chicken yard. The tale's proximate literary context is not limited to the *Monk's Tale*. It easily extends itself, through "wommanes conseil," to the *Tale of Melibee*. Through tragedy, eloquence, heroics, science, court flattery, courtly love, domesticity, dreams, scholarship, authority, antifeminism, patient humility and rural hullabaloo, there is scarcely a Chaucerian topic that is excluded from its purview and its criticism.

Unlike fable, the *Nun's Priest's Tale* does not so much make true and solemn assertions about life as it tests truths and tries out solemnities. If you are not careful, it will try out your solemnity too; it is here, doubtless, trying out mine. Some very great institutions lose importance in it, and some very humble ones are made magnificent. But considering Chaucer's reputation for satire and irony, the criticism in the tale needs less demonstration than does the wise conservatism that goes with it. The critical temper of the poem, unlike that of the *Merchant's Tale*, which is supported by a similar configuration of styles, produces no negative effect, but a continuously humane suggestion of the relativity of things. The shifting style and the succession of topics never rest long enough to serve a single view or a single doctrine or an unalterable judgment. Other tales adopt norms, then uncover differences according to their lights. This tale celebrates the normality of differences. If you take its humble, Griselda-like opening setting to represent a norm against which magnificence is satirized, you must reckon with the fox hunt that later turns the widow's dale and grove into a bedlam. Nor can you say that Chauntecleer and chickens in one perspective are not truly magnificent. None of the targets of the poem's parodies are demolished, or even really hit at the center. There are senses in which the solemnities of courtly love, science, marriage, authority, eloquence, tragedy, the Monk, and the *Tale of Melibee* are funny, but the *Nun's Priest's Tale* does not make us feel that they are always

funny. That would be the philosophy of the Cook, a fool who sees life as a continuous jape: "But God forbede that we stynte heere. . ." [3] The tale quite literally fulfills its prologue, which promises a merry tale *after* heaviness; it offers no conclusion but that sublunary values are comically unstable. The only absolute virtue that its reading educes is an enlightened recognition of the problem of perception itself, the virtue of seeing:

> "For he that wynketh, whan he sholde see,
> Al wilfully, God lat him nevere thee!" B 4622

The *Nun's Priest's Tale* is supremely Chaucerian in its poise before an overwhelming question. "What is this world?" That there is an absolute answer one can feel in the tacit security behind the Priest's humor, and in his sermonic conclusion:

> But ye that holden this tale a folye,
> As of a fox, or of a cok and hen,
> Taketh the moralite, goode men.
> For seint Paul seith that al that writen is,
> To oure doctrine it is ywrite, ywis;
> Taketh the fruyt, and lat the chaf be stille.
> Now, goode God, if that it be thy wille,
> As seith my lord, so make us alle goode men,
> And brynge us to his heighe blesse!
> Amen.   B 4636

His relativism is itself relative, and has its free play, after all, because he is talking about *this* world, not the other. But his piety is not, any more than are Chaucer's palinode and retraction, the main feature of his story. In the *Nun's Priest's Tale*, as altogether in the mature Chaucer, we are compelled to respect the conservative conclusion because the question has been so superbly well confronted. The tale's wit is, in little, the Chaucerian criticism; its forbearance is the Chaucerian tolerance. The Chaucerian mixed style illuminates the tale's microcosmic contradictions, just as it expresses, in large, the great capaciousness of Chaucer's humane vision.

[3] *Cook Prol* 4339.

Chaucer and the Fifteenth Century

IN THE HISTORY of the literature in English, Chaucer is an anomaly. He has no significant predecessors. His historical position could be plotted by reference to his contemporaries Gower, Langland, and the "Pearl" poet, and to Lydgate and the Scottish Chaucerians. But among the contemporaries, only Langland is comparable to him in realism and in complexity of style; the most Chaucerian of the others, William Dunbar, writes a full century later. Most of his followers see him only as the poet of high style:

> The noble rethor Poete of breteine
> That worthy was the laurer to haue
> Of peetrie and the palme atteine
> That made firste to distille and reyne
> The golde dewe droppis of speche and eloquence
> In-to our tounge . . .[4]

Chaucer's most illustrious admirer, Edmund Spenser, looks back to him from a distance of two centuries, and emulates him only faintly. English literature, then, for whatever the reasons, hardly provides us with a rich historical context for Chaucer's work, and it tends to promote a false idea of the novelty of his realism. In the preceding chapters I have suggested that Chaucer's position in literary history makes fuller sense if we consider him as belonging to that international, Gothic tradition of which French is the central literature. The earlier French tradition shows better than the English that Chaucer's realism is medieval, not modern or "Renaissance." It shows that his mixture of styles, rather than embodying some presumably advanced revolt from convention, is an expression of the very ambivalence of his culture, that it is the style of the period. Here I should like to indicate briefly and generally how the French tradition after Chaucer bears out these conclusions. The French literature of the fifteenth century does not of course

descend from Chaucer. The two belong, however, to the same tradition, and Chaucer's historical position is defined as well by the final phases of the tradition as by its beginnings.

By 1400 the high Gothic mode in every field had passed into a phase that is variously called "late," "baroque," "decadent," "flamboyant." [5] Late Gothic art represents an unbalance, a conflict, or a disintegration of elements that the high Gothic had held in momentary poise, and it has its own ostentatiousness which accentuates the lack of coherence. The fifteenth century saw, on the one hand, the continuation of the courtly tradition in a last stand of extravagant display. The age self-consciously perpetuated chivalry in social rituals, with processions and tournaments, the creation of knightly orders and cults of love. In literature, correspondingly, the tradition of romance and erotic allegory goes on unabated, and the courtly lyric is worked out in ever more diverse and sophisticated forms. As in England "the golde dewe droppis of speche and eloquence" are highly prized, so in France a school of *grands rhétoriqueurs* carries the practice of verbal ornament to ridiculous lengths. It is an age of extreme conventionalism in art. On the other hand, it is also an age of realism. Irrespective of whether the powerful, commercially interested middle class, despite its aping of the nobility, forced a material

---

[4] From John Lydgate, *The Life of Our Lady.*

[5] Franco-Burgundian art, literature, and culture of the late Middle Ages have been the subject of several excellent studies. The oversimple generalizations presented here are based largely on the observations of Huizinga, *Waning of the Middle Ages*; Auerbach, *Mimesis*, chap. X; Italo Siciliano, *François Villon et les thèmes poétiques du moyen âge* (Paris 1934) ; Henri Focillon, *Art d'occident* (Paris 1938) ; Erwin Panofsky, *Early Netherlandish Painting* (Cambridge, Mass., 1953) ; Helmut Hatzfeld, "Geist und Stil der flamboyanten Literatur in Frankreich," *Estudis Universitaris Catalans*, XXII (1936; Homenatje a Antonio Rubió i Lluch, III), 137–193.

view of things, or whether it was rather the nobility who now became aware of the shortcomings of chivalric idealism,[6] the fact is that the art of the period shows an extraordinary interest in everyday reality. Naturalism comes into its own in sculpture and painting. In literature the satiric-realistic tradition thrives, full of genre scenes and of intimate detailing of familiar speech and action. The earlier "bourgeois" frankness becomes more bold, with boisterousness, rawness, a crude sensualism and an impudent profanity.

These two sides of fifteenth-century culture exist together in varying relationships. In art, depending on the date, the field, and the man, naturalism can conceal a still highly worked symbolism, and chivalric ceremony can disguise a basic materialism and opportunism. Very often the mixture of styles is overt, based on the feudal distinction of class or just on transiency of mood. Whatever the manner of combination, however, an exaggerated Gothic dualism can be said to be a main trait of the style of the period. "All of the authors," it has been suggested, "have in some way or other the naturalistic view and the symbolic tradition as coördinates of their style." [7]

The decadence of late Gothic art, its excesses and defects of taste and form, is attributable to a loss of purposeful direction in the culture. Late medieval feudalism, whether courtly or religious, jealously preserved its forms and symbols, but could not perpetuate in depth its idealism. Late medieval realism, rapidly advancing in its capacity to see a naturalistic world and to represent it in art, was slow to acquire its own transcendentalism. The Renaissance was to recompose both motives in a new synthesis, but meanwhile transalpine culture seems to have been without moral underpinnings. Its symbolism is often merely gaud, its ceremony empty, its rhetoric only decorative. Its religion is incongruously

stretched between new ecstasies of mysticism and a profane, almost tactile familiarity with sacred matters. Its sense of fact is often spiritless or actually morbid. For all its boisterous play, the age is profoundly pessimistic; it is preoccupied with the irretrievable passage of time, with disorder, sickness, decay, and death.

Chaucer is eligible to be classed as a late Gothic poet for his range, for his mixture of styles, and for occasional passages in the fifteenth-century mood.[8] The *House of Fame* and the *Anelida* have the elaborateness and pointlessness, and some of the pessimism, of the later poetry. Chaucer's sentimental handling of maternal love and of little children is more of the fifteenth century than of earlier times. The unfinished *Cook's Tale* promises to have been the rawest of Chaucer's works. But these brushes with the possible dangers of his artistic and moral position serve to sharpen our notion of where Chaucer, in the main body of his works, actually stands. The feudal pageantry of the *Knight's Tale* could have, but did not, become the gratuitous and empty ceremonialism of the later *Jehan de Paris* and *Le Petit Jehan de Saintré*. The poem remains intensely moral; and its sense of chaos is bounded by a felt sense of order. Chaucer's Wife of Bath might have been given the decay of the flesh and the pessimism of Villon's *belle heaulmiere*.[9] Instead she has vitality and inextinguishable morale. No work of Chaucer's could more easily have become a document of decadence than his *Pardoner's Tale*. It contains the depth of cynicism, the dwelling on fleshly corruption and death, the flamboyant rhetoric, the circumstantial realism, the vulgarized allegory, the crudity, and the tastelessness of the late Gothic style. Yet none of these traits is finally gratuitous or uncon-

---

[6] Cf. Auerbach, *Mimesis*, 248–249; Huizinga, *Waning of the Middle Ages*, 115.
[7] Hatzfeld, "Geist und Stil," 185.

[8] Among the principal critics of Chaucer, Clemen seems to have been the only one who has been alert to the comparison. See *Der junge Chaucer*, esp. pp. 27–28, 142, 148–149, 170–172, 180, 201; cf. Hatzfeld, "Geist und Stil," pp. 163, 184.
[9] See François Villon, *Le Testament*, vv. 453–532.

trolled. Each is held in perspective: circumscribed by the larger scheme of the *Tales*, subsumed in the characterization of the Pardoner, bounded by the amicable ending, redeemed by the admission,

> And Jhesu Crist, that is our soules leche,
> So graunte yow his pardoun to receyve,
> For that is best.   C 918

The tale, while it explores the outermost limits of the medieval moral order, still proclaims the integrity of that order. This is the main difference between Chaucer and the literature of the French tradition in its decadence.

He is, then, supremely an artist of his own age. He does not announce the Renaissance, at least not any more than do medieval humanism and Gothic realism generally. He is not "modern": nowhere does he assert seriously and as final the primacy of realism in art, or the primacy of man or of matter in the universe. He is medieval. Nevertheless, his historical position is unique. His characteristic achievement as an artist is the holding together and seeing in relationship to each other of the wide range of values, some of them antithetical, which had once made up the richness and poise of medieval civilization, and were now already making for its break-up. He is, indeed, the culminating artist of the French tradition. No other poet in France or England, endowed with the variety, the disparity, the disorder of late medieval culture, sees it so clearly, embraces it so grandly, and masters it so well. In Europe Chaucer is the last medieval whose world is wide, yet still intelligible, viable, and one.

Wayne Shumaker

Alisoun in Wander-land: A Study in Chaucer's Mind and Literary Method

IN ONE of the best known of all the many books about Chaucer, John Livingston Lowes quoted anonymously a remark to the effect that realistic fiction of a recent period has a "fidelity, a life-likeness, a vividness, a touch, which are extraordinary and new" and then went on to say, "And yet—in certain qualities which we dub modern, Chaucer was as modern as the moderns, six centuries before their birth." [1]

The judgment is a familiar one, though it has been expressed in many different verbal formulas and with varying degrees of emphasis. The author of the *Wife of Bath's Prologue*, said R. K. Root, was "the first modern man of England, with the virtues and faults of our modern world." Percy Shelley declared that *"Troilus and Criseyde* and the *Canterbury Tales* represent an art that is modern rather than medieval." Agnes K. Getty, in a *PMLA* article entitled "The Mediaeval-Modern Conflict in Chaucer's Poetry," concluded that "Chaucer had, to a large extent, emerged from the influence of mediaeval literary technique in his last years." [2] It is hardly an exaggeration to say that the opinion stated with such confidence by Professor Lowes has become official. The belief that Chaucer was very much ahead of his time, that the patterns of thinking implicit in his later poems have a close

resemblance to those current in the nineteenth and twentieth centuries, appears to be widespread and authoritative.

When attempts have been made to substantiate this theory by argument and the citation of examples, the emphasis has regularly fallen, as in Professor Lowes' book, on Chaucer's "realism," his willingness to look at life directly instead of through the medium of books and literary conventions. "By degrees," wrote M. Legouis, summing up this part of the critical tradition still earlier in *A History of English Literature*, "he reached the point of deeming nothing as interesting and as diverse as Nature herself . . . He looked face to face at the spectacle of men and set himself to reproduce it directly. He made himself the painter of life." [3] No doubt some critics have dissented; it is not the custom for scholars in the humanities wholly to agree about any such generalization. Nevertheless the opinion that in his later poetry Chaucer relied heavily upon direct observation is at least highly respectable. Hence the judgment of his modernity. The modern artist is supposed to study the universe of sensory experience with great interest, whereas the medieval artist is thought to have conceived his works more abstractly, with reference to a whole system of ideal notions accepted for the most part on authority. Empirical art vs. metaphysical art: so the basic assumption underlying the view can be brief-

[1] *Geoffrey Chaucer and the Development of His Genius* (Boston, 1934), p. 185.
[2] The three quotations, respectively, are from *The Poetry of Chaucer* (Boston, 1922), p. 232; *The Living Chaucer* (Philadelphia, 1940), p. 43; and *PMLA* XLVII (1932), p. 402.

[3] New York, 1935 (translated by Helen Douglas Irvine), p. 156.

Reprinted by permission from *ELH*, XVIII (1951), 77–89.

ly stated. If the formulation is overly simple, it will serve all the more sharply to clarify the dichotomy implied by the judgments I have cited.

Now it is undeniable that persons and situations are often vividly enough evoked in Chaucer's later poetry to give the impression of having been directly observed. The Wife of Bath, especially, has been praised for her energetic *realness*. "Indubitably the most vigorous of Chaucer's creations"; "one of the two greatest and richest comic creations in English literature"; "the most vivid and detailed piece of character-drawing that Chaucer ever did": phrases like these about the Wife of Bath abound in critical literature.[4] I propose, accordingly, in the present article to examine Chaucer's treatment of the Wife in the hope of discovering how far the opinion of his modernity is justified. This will require that we look rather carefully at the *Wife's Prologue* and a part of the *General Prologue,* but not at all at the *Wife's Tale,* which has no bearing upon the point at issue.

II

In many respects the Wife of Bath is very far removed from the personages in Chaucer's earlier, admittedly medieval, poetry. She breathes a different air, inhabits a different world: so, at least, we feel as we hear her vigorously defending her very earthy thesis that marriage is lawful and that within it authority should be wielded, or rather flourished, by the wife. She seems to us "real," not a type, and a few attentive readings prepare us to be convinced by Professor Manly that she was drawn from a living original.

All the details which distinguish her from other lusty women contribute to the impression. At the time of her marriage she

[4] I take the phrases, respectively, from Legouis, *op. cit.,* p. 153; B. J. Whiting *et al., The College Survey of English Literature* (New York, 1942), I, 171; and J. S. P. Tatlock, *The Development and Chronology of Chaucer's Works* (London, 1907), p. 210.

was not simply "young," but twelve years old. She had not "several" husbands, but five, not to speak of other company in youth. Of the five two were bad and three good, rich, and old. Her fifth husband was named Jankyn and had once been a clerk at Oxford. She was on good terms with her niece and had a gossip whose name was the same as her own. The occasion on which she and Jankyn had such fine dalliance in the field that she was moved virtually to propose to him came during a Lent. Jankyn's age when she admired his clean legs as he walked behind her fourth husband's bier was twenty, she then being forty or older. Her deafness was caused by the same man's having struck her on the ear after she had torn a leaf from one of his books. If we add to these and other similarly precise bits of information given us by Alys herself the further details provided earlier by the *General Prologue*—the location of her home, her florid complexion, the color of her hose, the hugeness of her hat, the nature of her dentition, the excellence of her wimpling, and so on—the portrait which finally emerges is remarkable for its roundness and the vividness of its coloring. The very manner and rhythm of her speech, so racy and idiosyncratic, with lost threads and sudden reversals of direction, individualize her and seem to put her on quite a different plane from Blanche, in the *Book of the Duchess,* or even Dorigen, in the *Franklin's Tale.* She is less remote, less ideal, less abstract—in a word, more actual.

And yet there is another and opposite side to the Wife of Bath, one equally important technically and, I believe, just now in greater need of being stressed. The best way I know of approaching it is rather circuitous, through the consideration of an aspect of her experiences that has been little discussed.

The curiosity of many readers must have been piqued by the lines in the *General Prologue* in which Chaucer says of the Wife of Bath that

thries hadde she been at Jerusalem;
She hadde passed many a straunge strem;
At Rome she hadde been, and at Boloigne,
In Galice at Seint Jame, and at Coloigne.
She koude muchel of wandrynge by the
weye.   A 467

I wish for a time to play with the idea that Alisoun, or Alys, as for the sake of brevity I prefer to call her, really made the pilgrimages enumerated here. There is a possibility that such a person did, for other scholars than Professor Manly have believed her to be drawn from life, and Chaucer may well have heard her boast about the length and frequency of her travels or mention incidents which had occurred on them. Later we shall consider the effect on the argument of the other possibilities: that she had a living prototype who did not make the pilgrimages, and that she had no living prototype, or so many that as she exists in the pages of the *Canterbury Tales* she may be considered essentially imaginary and non-historical. But first let us entertain the idea I have suggested. The reason for doing so will become apparent later.

If Alys did travel thrice to the Holy Land (I say nothing of her shorter pilgrimages), her mind must have been richly stocked with memories. What some of the memories were can be guessed from an account of a nearly contemporary pilgrimage to Jerusalem made by Margery Kempe, also a married Englishwoman whose financial circumstances seem to have been roughly similar to Alys'. The journey described in *The Book of Margery Kempe* was apparently made between 1413 and 1415—that is to say, long before there had been any important changes in conditions of travel or the state of the shrines along the way and in Palestine. Much of what Margery saw must also have been seen by Alys, and the inconveniences and dangers along the route must often have been the same for both.

For example, there were the Palestinian shrines themselves, the holiest in Christendom and full of awe for every Christian.

The emotional atmosphere in which the Church of the Holy Sepulcher was viewed is well suggested by Margery. Plenary indulgence was granted at four spots within the Church's precincts, the Mount of Calvary, Christ's tomb, the Stone of Unction, and the place where the cross had been buried. Pilgrims regularly spent an entire night in worship at these and other altars in order fully to savor the significance of what they saw.

Than went þei to þe Tempyl in Ierusalem, & þei wer latyn in on þe to day at evynsong-tyme & abydyn þer-in til þe next day at euynsong-tyme. þan þe frerys [Franciscans] lyftyd up a cros & led þe pylgrimys a-bowte fro [on] place to an-oþer wher owyr Lord had sufferyd hys [peynys] and hys passyons, euery man & woman beryng a wax candel in her hand. & þe frerys al-wey, as þei went a-bowte, teld hem what owyr Lord sufferyd in euery place. & þe forseyd creatur wept & sobbyd so plentyvowsly as þow sche had seyn owyr Lord wyth hir bodyly ey sufferyng hys Passon at þat tyme. [5]

Though Alys was no doubt less susceptible than Margery, she too was a Christian ("We leven alle," said the Shipman, "in the grete God"), [6] and must have been deeply impressed. The rocky hillock thought to be Golgotha, the hole said to have received the foot of the cross, the spot where the nails were driven through Christ's shrinking hands and feet, the Chapel of the Holy Sepulcher, the burial-place of the cross, the Chapel of the Apparition of Jesus to His Mother on Easter Day, and the Stone of Unction could hardly have been viewed with indifference. Margery was so affected that she wept and sobbed almost continuously; and on Calvary she first began to "cry" in the boisterous manner which for ten years afterwards made bitter enemies

---

[5] *The Book of Margery Kempe*, ed. Sanford Brown Meech and Hope Emily Allen (Oxford University Press, 1940), pp. 67–68.
[6] *Epilogue of the Man of Law's Tale*, 1181. For all quotations from Chaucer I use F. N. Robinson's Student's Cambridge Edition (Boston, 1933).

and caused her to be ejected from churches as a public nuisance.

sche fel down þat sche mygth not stondyn ne knelyn but walwyd & wrestyd wyth hir body, spredyng hir armys a-brode, & cried wyth a lowde voys as þow hir hert xulde a brostyn a-sundyr, for in þe cite of hir sowle sche saw veryly & freschly how owyr Lord was crucifyed. [7]

Someone in Alys' party may have been similarly affected. If so, the sobs and tears would have become a part of Alys' experience of the shrines and contributed to its vividness. But these are only a few of the places in the vicinity that Alys must have visited. If she took the usual tours she walked the Via Dolorosa and saw, among other memorable show-places, Mount Zion, the Pentecostal Chamber, the place of the Virgin's burial, the Church of the Nativity in Bethlehem, the River Jordan (where the sands were so hot that Margery "wend hir feet schuld a brent"), the Mount Quarentine, the birthplace of John the Baptist, Bethany, "þer Mary & Martha dwellyd," the grave of Lazarus, the spot "þer Mary Mawdelyn stode when Crist seyd to hir, 'Mary, why wepyst þu?' " and "many mo placys þan be wretyn." [8]

Rome also was full of temples and shrines, and the probability is strong that Alys' visit to Rome was made on her return from the Holy Land, just as was Margery's. But instead of speaking further of the holy places which were the ostensible (and often the real) objects of the pilgrimages I wish to suggest briefly the circumstances in which Alys passed her strange streams and gained her knowledge of wandering by the way. The travels required much more time than the sightseeing tours and were perhaps even more productive of unforgettable memories. For when travel was not tamed by modern conveniences—I am thinking of spring-leafed carriages and turnpikes as well as of trains, motor ships,

and airplanes—a trip through a foreign land brought one into contact with the exotic people and countryside to an extent not easily conceivable today.

For one thing, progress was very slow, and one had ample time to become accustomed to the changes from a familiar environment. We are to imagine Alys as progressing southeastward from England at the rate, possibly, of ten to thirty miles a day, riding horseback or drawn sometimes in a wagon or cart, and in due time returning northwestward at the same rate; but even this progress was broken by long stops whenever it became necessary to wait for a ship or arrange to accompany a different party. Margery had to wait twelve weeks at Venice for a galley to take her down the Adriatic to Palestine.[9] And the environment must have changed constantly. There was as yet no large-scale industry and therefore, of course, no standardization. One did not, as today, continue everywhere in the civilized world to eat very much the same food and sleep in almost identical hotels. If Alys had any housewifely instincts at all she must have watched with interest the variations in the foods spread out for sale in the successive markets and observed from her vantage-point on horseback, sometimes with envy and sometimes with disdain, the un-English furnishings of the houses along village and city streets. Almost certainly she had a sharp eye for women's fashions. Unless I misread her character, however, it would have been her fellow-pilgrims who fascinated her most. They would have been natives of many different countries who spoke a varied assortment of languages and had widely divergent habits and attitudes. And her opportunities of becoming intimately acquainted with them, so far as verbal communication was possible directly or through interpreters, would have been excellent. The group would

[7] *Book of Margery Kempe*, p. 68.
[8] The first of the quoted phrases is from p. 74, the remaining three from p. 75.

[9] The stay may have been pleasant. Professor Meech quoted a remark from an anonymous itinerary to the effect that "The abidyng atte Venyse in wynter is goodly." See his note on p. 65.

have eaten together, stopped in the same inns, perhaps have taken lodgings together in Venice or Rome, and, almost literally, have slept together. (One remembers the sleeping accommodations in the *Reve's Tale*.) And all this for months on end—possibly, so far as some individuals were concerned, for a year or more. Margery's single trip to Palestine required more than a year and a half. Alys made three trips, and though she may have dawdled less than Margery, whose oddities of manner necessitated frequent changes of companions, it is reasonable to estimate that at least three of her most vigorous and observant years were spent outside England.

The spectacle of English wayfaring life has been elaborately described by M. Jusserand, and I need not try to evoke similar pictures of roadside activities on the continent and in the Near East. I may point out, however, that the Hundred Years' War spanned Alys' lifetime as it did Margery's; she too may have passed through territories which were in armed dispute. Margery once says, "þer was opyn werr be-twix þe English and þo cuntreys, þerfor hir drede was meche þe mor."[10] The roads over which she passed must also have been infested by miserable and dangerous people like the beggars Margery once joined en route to Calais: "powr folke," she charitably called them, who stripped themselves between towns and sat naked to pick the lice out of their clothing.[11] If Alys ever became separated from her party, as Margery several times did, she too may have begged permission to sleep on "an hep of brakys [ferns] in an hows," while her companion lay down gratefully in a barn.[12]

If there were space I should like to speak of travel by sea: of the layman's usual fear of ships, the consequent avoidance of water whenever there was an alternate land route, the danger of piracy (as of robbery

ashore), the fetid holds of Venetian galleys, the promotion of intimate companionship by crowded berthing facilities, the probability that sometimes, when the seas were smooth and the air mild, Alys heard educated fellow-voyagers expatiate on the influence of stars visible from the weatherdeck. But I have said all I now can and must return to Chaucer and his narrative methods.

If I have been at all successful in my intention, the Wife's travels now lie somewhat less dormantly in the reader's consciousness than if I had not undertaken the foregoing brief summary. It would have been simpler, but I think in the present context inadequate, to say, "Consider how many interesting experiences Alys must have had on her pilgrimages." No images would have risen in the imagination; there would have been no automatic awareness of what such ambitious journeyings meant in the fourteenth century in time, inconvenience, actual danger, and compensatory satisfactions. My purpose requires that the pilgrimages exist as more than a half-dozen colorless words in the *General Prologue*, for I intend to push their importance to the *Wife's Prologue* very hard.

If, as Professors Manly and Robinson, among others, have believed, Alys had a flesh-and-blood prototype whom Chaucer knew, and if in reporting Alys' words he drew, at least for her *Prologue*, on what he had heard the living Wife say, it is highly probable that there will have crept into her autobiographical discourse some references to the experiences concerning which we have partly informed ourselves. It is scarcely credible that the holiest altars in Christendom, the strange streams and ways, the foreign inns and exotic customs, the unfamiliar foodstuffs and household economies, the ships and varying seas, and, most of all, the wonderfully diverse *people* among whom her travels threw her for long periods of time would have left no traces in her conversation. A woman who insisted, as we know Alys did, on going first to the

---

[10] *Ibid.*, p. 232. This and the following two references are not to the Palestinian pilgrimage.
[11] *Ibid.*, p. 237.
[12] *Ibid.*, p. 240.

offering was not likely to play down any of her valid claims to distinction. Moreover, the rambling structure of her *Prologue* is ideally suited to the introduction of foreign reminiscences, and her theme one which would be illuminated by observations on continental and Eastern practices. And we know (still on the assumption that the Wife was historical) that she did actually speak of her pilgrimages, for in the *General Prologue* Chaucer shows himself to have been impressed by them. He knew not only of the long trips to Palestine but also of three shorter and much less noteworthy journeys, to the shrine of the Virgin at Boulogne-sur-Mer (if Robinson's conjecture is right), that of Saint James at Compostella, and that of the Three Kings at Cologne. Alys' mind was neither factual nor systematic. I take it accordingly that she did not count off the pilgrimages on her fingers and leave the matter there.

The theory of the prototype is attractive —indeed, to me, convincing—because no alternative hypothesis accounts so satisfactorily for the Wife's genesis in the literary *milieu* of the late fourteenth century. (The same reasoning applies with somewhat lesser force to the Host, the Cook, and some of the other pilgrims.) But my train of thought does not depend on the Wife's having been sketched from life. Anyhow, it is unthinkable that Chaucer did not feel free to make whatever changes in her character and history his aesthetic purpose demanded. If she was wholly imaginary, or so varied from one living original, or several, that her travels were purely fictive, the presumption is surely that the fiction was calculated to further the achievement of a poetic aim. And if the aim, whether conscious or unconscious, was to paint a lifelike, vivid, convincing individual—in modern critical jargon, to *realize* a delightful Wife of Bath—then we have a right to expect Chaucer to have turned the suggestion of travels to account in Alys' long monologue. His acquaintance with foreign peoples and settings was intimate enough to

enable him to do so effectively. If this was not his intention at the time he wrote the *General Prologue*, one is at a loss to explain the presence of the five lines naming the pilgrimages. In themselves the lines have little vivifying force. If they arouse a vague excitement, the reason is that they hint at events about which we are immediately curious to know more.

Thus both lines of reasoning lead to the same expectation. I say nothing of the structural necessity that all the important foreshadowings in the *General Prologue* be fully bodied out later, for the *Canterbury Tales* are after all only a splendid fragment. I am content to emphasize the magnificent opportunities laid open by the mention of extended travels in the preliminary character-sketch. If, as we have been led to believe by Professor Lowes and others, Chaucer was genuinely interested in the sharp evocation of people and situations, the Wife's long speech in her *Prologue* will make capital of the pilgrimages. If it does not, the reason will certainly be that before writing the *Prologue* Chaucer discovered even greater potentialities for evocation in other blocks of aesthetic material.

The expectation is almost entirely disappointed. Only two unmistakable references to the pilgrimages can be found, and of these one ("He deyde whan I cam fro Jerusalem") simply places an event in time and is no way explored. The second has a somewhat greater compositional importance.

> What wiste I wher my grace
> Was shapen for to be, or in what place?
> Therfore I made my visitaciouns
> To vigilies and to processiouns,
> To prechyng eek, and to thise pilgrimages,
> To pleyes of myracles, and to mariages.   D 558

But this passage does no more than show us rather casually that the foreign pilgrimages were consistent with Alys' total character. It throws a light backwards on the character-sketch without capitalizing on the opportunities for realization of situation and incident. The suggestions of Alys' lusty sexual appetites in the *General Prologue* are picked up and worked out with consummate skill. Not so the remarks about the travels. Neither are greater potentialities for evocation in other kinds of materials exploited. Instead we are given something qualitatively quite different.

That something is an almost endless series of quotations from the Authorities. Alys, like Chanticleer, Prudence, and all sorts of other improbable people and animals (chiefly birds), is made a storehouse of medieval learning. In the eight hundred twenty-eight lines of her *Prologue* she refers with the self-confident assurance of a scholar to Jesus, Solomon, St. Paul, Lamech, Abraham, Jacob, Mark, Ptolemy, Argus, Job, Metellius, Venus, Darius, Appelles, Mars, Simplicius Gallus, Ecclesiastes, Valerius, Theophrastus, Jerome, Jovinian, Tertullian, Chrysippus, Trotula, Héloise, Ovid, Midas, Adam, Mercury, Eve, Sampson, Hercules, Dejanira, Socrates, Xantippe, Pasiphaë, Clytemnestra, Amphiaraus, Eriphyle, Livia, Lucilia, Latumyus (whoever he is), and Arrius, not to mention the various saints by whom she swears—an average of better than one new literary or mythological reference to every twenty lines. This is to say that instead of allowing the Wife to use personal materials Chaucer requires her to use impersonal ones—the stock-in-trade of every good medieval student. Instead of permitting her to be herself, he sets her up, red hose, widely-spaced teeth, moist shoes, enormous hat, and all the rest, as a blue-stocking (if I may be permitted a play on colors), quite as thoroughly at home among classical and patristic authors as he was himself.

It will not do to brush aside all this amassing of texts and *exempla* with a wave of the hand and the utterance of the magical word "Irony." Of course the assigning of all this unlikely information to the Wife is a joke. But more is involved than humor. The Authorities are omnipresent in Chaucer, in his most deeply serious works as well

as in his most light-hearted and raucous stories. They are one mark of his "medievalism," his deference to the ideal notions we were given the impression he had abandoned. And having said so much, I must follow the line of argument to the end and assert that nowhere in the *Canterbury Tales* does Chaucer commit himself utterly to an exploration of the implications of personality. He adapts the tales to their tellers. He invents excuses for introducing the literary citations of which he was so fond, as when he pretends that Alys is repeating what her fifth husband had read to her. He sometimes slyly uses his learning as it would have been used by one of his pilgrims had the pilgrim been able to possess it. He shows an extraordinary and precious awareness of idiosyncratic appearance and behavior. But he does not, except by way of introduction in the *General Prologue*, keep the focus very long upon *men*. About the intellectual and emotional tensions that underlie outward eccentricity he knows chiefly what an impersonal medieval science and philosophy have taught him. More important still, he does not seek tirelessly by direct observation to learn more. He has no really profound curiosity about the individual soul. His strongest interest is in the general—in what is not (as it would have seemed to him) self-limiting and therefore trivial. He is not a patient searcher of men's hearts, but a docile scholar who imposes upon his perceptions, as scholars have always tended to do, a framework of systematized notions.

In this way, no doubt, he saw Alys of Bath: at first, delightedly, with his physical eyes and instinctive sympathies; later with the eye of inward vision, which strove to find in her a representative of something larger and more important than herself.

III

I wish to make it quite clear that I do not condemn Chaucer for failing to do what was neither customary nor philosophically necessary for fourteenth-century writers. Since the will was thought to be a more important part of character than the modifications of attitude and habit induced by environmental circumstances, it was not necessary for a poet to follow out with meticulous care, as a modern novelist would do, the psychological consequences of every action he admitted into his story. On the contrary, he preferred to show triumphantly the ability of the soul to rise above circumstances. Chaucer's Constance, his Prudence, his St. Cecilia, and his Griselda—precisely the characters of whom he continued to approve at the time of his retraction—all exemplify the power of a strong will to maintain its poise despite crushing calamities. What counted in the Christian view of life was not that the spirit sometimes breaks under pressure, but that it sometimes magnificently preserves its integrity. As a devout Christian, Chaucer shared the view, and twentieth-century readers cannot intelligently reproach him with holding it.

Indeed, one may take the opposite view and point out that his assumptions made possible the achievement of literary values for which writers today strive against infinitely greater difficulties. To the twentieth century the universe seems in some respects much more inscrutable than it did to Chaucer and his contemporaries. If we know more about physical laws, Chaucer knew more about the ultimate meanings of phenomena. He knew, particularly, that ultimate meanings are limited in number, and he therefore had a confidence we cannot have that by scrutiny in the light of abstract principles any subject could be portrayed in its universal aspects. He was not, like so many educated people today, a practical solipsist, satisfied with an interpretation of life that is personally adequate. The habit of his mind was to work from discrete human situations toward something broader. He reached, that is to say, for a universal. And if the Wife of Bath has sometimes been hailed as the incarnation of an eternal tendency in womankind, the reason is partly that Chaucer has not been satisfied to leave her an individual.

We need not, of course, choose between the individual and typical interpretations. Alys is both woman and women. But if some necessity were put upon us to impoverish our reading of her *Prologue* by denying one set of her qualities, I believe Chaucer would prefer us to relinquish her individuality.

John Speirs

from The *Canterbury Tales*

THE *Canterbury Tales* is the completion of Chaucer's poetry; it was his work in the last decade of the fourteenth century and of his life. One or two of the tales are, or appear to be, early. But the great Prologue, the interludes between the tales and the majority of the tales are unmistakably the creation of Chaucer's fullest maturity.

In relation to the planned whole, the work is a succession of fragments. The position of the great Prologue is, of course, not in doubt. Nor is there any doubt that the first tale was intended to be the Knight's, and that it was to be succeeded by the Miller's, the Reve's and the Cook's. After this first group there is a break. The *Canterbury Tales* consists of several such groups which had evidently not been placed in any final order when Chaucer died. Yet the impression the great poem leaves upon the mind is anything but that of a fragmentary work; it is a poem complete in itself as an impression of the diversity and plenitude of human life—"God's plenty."

In the *Canterbury Tales* narrative art is at the point of becoming drama. The poem is the culmination of Chaucer's dramatic-poetic development of English speech; and something unaccountably *new* in mediaeval literature. The *personae* are first presented in the great Prologue with a vividness not attained before in English, even by Chaucer, and seldom since. Thereafter, in the comic interludes between the tales, they begin to move and talk and act. The Wife of Bath's preamble—which is twice the length of her tale—is the Wife herself talking, enacting scenes and dialogues between herself and her several husbands, dramatizing her private life in front of an audience;

her tale itself is the Wife continuing to talk. The Pardoner's Prologue and Tale are another character's self-dramatization. The *Canterbury Tales* thus presents a company of distinct and individual people talking; the tales are a part of themselves and their talk. The interest is not simply in the tale —vivid as it nearly always is in itself—but, at the same time, in the teller and in the tale as characteristic of the teller. The variety of the tales reproduces and fulfils the initial human variety. Each tale dramatically projects a distinct person. It is hard for us to credit (after it has happened) how new were the possibilities realized for the first time in the *Canterbury Tales*; the poem is the beginning of English dramatic and fictional literature as a whole. The "so seemingly unstudied" [1] technical accomplishment of the great Prologue, the comic interludes and the maturest tales is the fulfilment of a process of experiment and exploration which was more than technical; it is an aspect of the depth and maturity of Chaucer's daringly achieved vision of human life.

The *Canterbury Tales* is the Human Comedy of the Middle Ages. Dante's *Divine Comedy* is a rationally ordered vision of the *moral* universe. In the *Inferno* the categories of evil, as Dante had particularly experienced and identified these in his Italy, are each apprehended and placed according to its degree. By way of the *Purgatorio* the ascent is made through the intervening planes of being, to the climax of the *Paradiso*. Dante thus, in a single vision, comprehends man in the multiplicity of his re-

[1] Coleridge.

Reprinted by permission from John Speirs, *Chaucer the Maker*, London, Faber and Faber, revised edition, 1960, pp. 97–99, 168–177.

lationship to God—through each of the spheres of moral being, from states of perdition (or utter deprivation of God) to the higher and highest states of beatitude (or contemplative love of God). In the *Canterbury Tales* the object of the poet's contemplation is the human order as in itself it is, having its place in a divinely established natural order; it is presented as immediately as it presented itself to Chaucer's alert perception in his contemporary England. The procession of Chaucer's Canterbury pilgrims is the procession of the Human Comedy. It is *Le Pèlerinage de la Vie Humaine* (as Blake recognized, it has both a timeless and a temporal aspect. "They are the physiognomies and lineaments of universal human life.")

> This world nis but a thurghfare ful of wo,
> And we ben pilgrimes, passinge to and
>   fro.   A 2848

But the tone of Chaucer's company of English folk is as a whole one of jollity; and, scandalously careless in relation to eternity as several of the company appear to be, this jollity accords with the tone of grateful acceptance of life which is the tone of the *Canterbury Tales* as a whole. The *personae* of the comedy are so vivid that we feel them (as Dryden did) to be our immediate contemporaries and are apt to miss the depth of difference of their background; yet it is that unfamiliar depth which lends the vivid comedy its richer significance. A way of life, a whole phase of civilization different in many respects from our own— though our own has evolved from it—goes to the composing of that Chaucerian depth. The human comedy of the *Canterbury Tales* moves within an apprehension of an all-inclusive divine harmony. There is no mitigation of the evil in the Canterbury pilgrims nor in the characters of their tales; indeed, the rogues and scoundrels have been remarked to predominate in the *Canterbury Tales*. Yet the divine order—in relation to which we are all judged—is not felt to be disturbed, and the contemplation

of even the "evil" characters is correspondingly steady. Life in its totality—both "good" and "evil"—is accepted as exactly what it is observed to be.

*   *   *   *   *   *   *   *   *

THE PHYSICIAN'S TALE, THE PARDONER'S PROLOGUE AND TALE

There is again a break after the *Franklin's Tale*. The *Physician's Tale* and the *Pardoner's Prologue* and *Tale* follow in the best MSS.; and these, wherever they would finally have stood in relation to the other tales, are expressly intended to stand together. The *Pardoner's Prologue* and *Tale* are organically one, a dramatization of the Pardoner, and unmistakably one of Chaucer's maturest achievements.

The *Physician's Tale*—the tale of Apius and Virginia—reads not unlike one of the legends of the *Legend of Good Women*, and may well have been composed contemporaneously with these. This tale of a virgin killed by her father to preserve her virginity—a martyrdom for virginity—is left relatively undeveloped by Chaucer, though it is lent some human interest by him as a tale of a false judge and the tragedy of a father and daughter.

But the Chaucerian dramatic interest here is less in the tale itself than in the Host's reaction to it. The good-natured fellow is powerfully affected, his Englishman's sense of justice outraged.

> "Harrow!" quod he, "by nayles and by blood!
> This was a fals cherl and a fals
>   justyse! . . ."   C 289

He declares he is in need of a drink to restore his spirits, or else of a merry tale; so he calls upon the Pardoner. At that the "gentils" are fearful of hearing some "ribaudye" and insist "Tel us som moral thing." The Pardoner has, as he says, to "thinke up-on som honest thing" while he drinks. The irony is that he does indeed tell a moral tale with a vengeance.

But first, after this interlude, comes the *Pardoner's Prologue* to his *Tale*. This consists, as he drinks, of his "confession"—a "confession" of the same order as that of the Wife of Bath. The "confession" should simply be accepted as a convention like those soliloquies in Elizabethan plays in which the villain comes to the front of the stage and, taking the audience entirely into his confidence, unmasks himself ("I am determined to prove a villain"). The consideration that the rogue is here apparently giving away to his fellow-pilgrims the secrets he lives by will only intervene when we refuse (incapacitated, perhaps, by modern "naturalistic" conventions) to accept the convention—and that would be just as unreasonable as if we were to refuse to accept the other convention that he speaks in verse. Even by "naturalistic" expectations the phenomenon is not outrageously improbable. In an excess of exhibitionism, glorying and confident in his invincible roguery, his tongue loosened by drink, the Pardoner is conceivable as sufficiently carried away to boast incautiously as well as impudently. But such considerations are hardly the relevant ones here. A conventionalized dramatic figure—such as could not be met with off a stage—is not necessarily less living or less of a reality than a purely "naturalistic" dramatic figure. That partly depends on the vitality of the convention itself, which may concentrate instead of dissipate, eliminate all but essentials, sharply define, focus and intensify. Within the frame of the present convention—the "confession"—a dramatization of spectacular boldness, remarkable intensity and even subtlety is presented. By its means the Pardoner exhibits himself (like the Wife of Bath) without reserve.

The themes of the Pardoner's initial characterization in the great *Prologue* are developed and illustrated dramatically in both the *Pardoner's Prologue* and his *Tale,* which together may be regarded as all the Pardoner's monologue. He combines several roles. His chief role, in which he most prides himself, is that of the fraudulent preacher who preaches against the sin which he himself typifies—Avarice. The object of his emotional and vivid sermons against Avarice is to loosen his hearers' heart-strings and purse-strings for his own profit. To this immoral end he is consciously the declamatory preacher, the spellbinder, in the guise of holiness. He presents, for admiration, the image of himself in the pulpit, incidentally revealing his contempt for the "lewed peple" whom he deceives.

I peyne me to han an hauteyn speche,
And ringe it out as round as gooth a
belle . . .   C 331
I stonde lyk a clerk in my pulpet,
And whan the lewed peple is doun y-set,
I preche, so as ye han herd bifore,
And telle an hundred false japes more.
Than peyne I me to strecche forth the nekke,
And est and west up-on the peple I bekke,
As doth a dowve sitting on a berne.
Myn hondes and my tonge goon so yerne,
That it is joye to see my bisinesse.
Of avaryce and of swich cursednesse
Is al my preching, for to make hem free
To yeve her pens, and namely un-to
me . . .   402
I rekke never, whan that they ben beried,
Though that her soules goon a-blake-
beried!   406

He will do no honest work (such as weave baskets). His other profitable roles are those of a pedlar of pardons and sham relics, and a medicine-man selling false remedies and formulas to induce people to feel and believe what they would like to —against the evidence of their own senses —and to multiply the crops and cure sick animals.

For, though a man be falle in jalous rage,
Let maken with this water his potage,
And never shal he more his wyf mistriste,
Though he the sooth of hir defaute wiste;
Al had she taken preestes two or three.
Heer is a miteyn eek, that ye may see,
He that his hond wol putte in this miteyn,
He shal have multiplying of his
greyn . . .   C 374

Part of the power he exerts is unmistakably as a survival of the traditional medicine-man. As the eternal charlatan, show-man or quack, his roles are still being played not only in market-places and at street corners.

The *Pardoner's Tale* has the dual character of a popular sermon and a moral tale. The tale itself is such as might have been grafted on to a popular sermon on Gluttony and Avarice as an *exemplum*, to show Death as the wages of sin. It belongs (though in its origins clearly an old traditional tale) with the Pardoner's own preaching as he has been describing and enacting it in his *Prologue*. But the order by which the tale is subsidiary to the sermon is in this case reversed. Instead of the tale growing out of the sermon, the sermon here grows out of the tale; instead of incorporating the tale, the sermon is here incorporated in the tale; and the tale concludes, not only with a final condemnation of the sins of Gluttony and Avarice, but a confident attempt by the Pardoner to make the most of its terrifying effect by yet another production of the scandalous bulls and relics. The Pardoner's preaching and entertaining are entangled, perhaps confused in his own mind, share an identical lurid life, and are calculated by him to promote his private business ends.

The lurid opening of the tale startles us sensationally into attention with its images of ferocious riot, and with the tone of moral indignation which accompanies these images, a moral indignation that on examination turns out (as frequently with moral indignation) not to be so moral after all, but to be itself an accompanying emotional orgy on the part of the Pardoner.

> . . yonge folk, that haunteden folye,
> As ryot, hasard, stewes, and tavernes,
> Wher-as, with harpes, lutes, and giternes,
> They daunce and pleye at dees both day and
>   night,
> And ete also and drinken over hir might,
> Thurgh which they doon the devel sacrifyse
> With-in that develes temple, in cursed wyse,
> By superfluitee abhominable;
> Hir othes been so grete and so dampnable,
> That it is grisly for to here hem swere;

> Our blissed lordes body they to-tere;
> Hem thoughte Jewes rente him noght y-nough;
> And ech of hem at otheres sinne lough.
> And right anon than comen tombesteres
> Fetys and smale, and yonge fruytesteres,
> Singers with harpes, baudes, wafereres,
> Whiche been the verray develes officeres
> To kindle and blowe the fyr of lecherye,
> That is annexed un-to glotonye;
> That holy writ take I to my witnesse,
> That luxurie is in wyn and dronkenesse.   C 484

The images are presented along with a thunderous over-charge of shocked and outraged half-superstitious, half-religious feeling.

> . . . they doon the devel sacrifyse
> With-in that develes temple, in cursed wyse.

Blasphemy is visualized as an act monstrously unnatural and ghastly, the mutilation of the body of Christ.

Our imagination having been seized by these sensational means we find ourselves launched first not into a tale but into a sermon. This "digression"—a sermon on gluttony and drunkenness, gambling and swearing—again serves an integrating and dramatic function. Not only are the themes of the sermon themes which the suspended tale will illustrate, but the sermon is a further exhibition by the Pardoner of his powers, and a further revelation of the Pardoner. He consciously dramatizes certain aspects of himself—he is a play actor by nature and profitable practice—but is unconscious of other aspects of himself. He is both half-horrified and half-fascinated by the subject matter of his sermon. He unconsciously gloats over the sins he zestfully condemns. There is in his sermon (as, Eliot remarks, perhaps lurks even in some of Donne's sermons on corruption) a sly yielding to what for him is the grotesque fascination of the flesh. The dramatization here is more inclusive than the Pardoner's own conscious self-dramatization as a popular preacher, and it completely detaches and objectifies even the sermon as comic dramatic art.

After a succession of popular *ensamples* from the Bible, the Pardoner in his sermon dwells on the original instance of "glotonye"—the eating of the forbidden fruit by Adam and his wife—and this produces a succession of indignant (or mock-indignant) apostrophes and exclamations— "O glotonye . . . O glotonye. . . ."

> Allas! the shorte throte, the tendre mouth,
> Maketh that, Est and West, and North and South,
> In erthe, in eir, in water men to-swinke
> To gete a glotoun deyntee mete and drinke! C 520

The idea corresponds to the Jacobean idea that the fine clothes on a courtier's or lady's back may have cost an estate—evidence again that the Jacobean social conscience was inherited from the mediaeval religious attitude. The poetry here depends particularly on the contrasts arising from the conjunction of vigorous popular speech with scholastic phraseology.

> O wombe! O bely! O stinking cod,
> Fulfild of donge and of corrupcioun!
> At either ende of thee foul is the soun.
> How greet labour and cost is thee to finde!
> Thise cokes, how they stampe, and streyne, and grinde,
> And turnen substaunce in-to accident,
> To fulfille al thy likerous talent!
> Out of the harde bones knokke they
> The mary, for they caste noght a-wey
> That may go thurgh the golet softe and swote. C 543

A fantastic-comic effect is produced by the virtual dissociation of the belly and the gullet—as, just before, of the throat and mouth—from the rest of the body, their virtual personification and consequent magnification; and by the impression of the wasted labour and sweat of the cooks in (contrasting metaphysical phrase) "turnen substaunce in-to accident." The vigorous coarseness and the metaphysics come together, momentarily, in the term "corrupcioun." How close Chaucer can sometimes come, in some of the elements of his art, to the vernacular sermons, and *Piers Plowman* is once again shown in the Pardoner's farcical impression of Drunkenness.

> O dronke man, disfigured is thy face,
> Sour is thy breeth, foul artow to embrace,
> And thurgh thy dronke nose semeth the soun
> As though thou seydest ay "Sampsoun, Sampsoun";
> And yet, god wot, Sampsoun drank never no wyn.
> Thou fallest, as it were a stiked swyn . . . C 556
> That whan a man hath dronken draughtes three,
> And weneth that he be at hoom in Chepe,
> He is in Spayne, right at the toune of Lepe,
> Nat at the Rochel, ne at Burdeux toun;
> And thanne wol he seye, "Sampsoun, Sampsoun." 572

Gluttony has been visualized in the sermon as parts of the body that have taken on a kind of independent life of their own as in the fable of the rebellious members; drunkenness is impersonated realistically as a drunk man.

The tavern scene is before us again—on the resumption of the suspended tale—and has as its sombre and sinister background one of those periodic visitations of the pestilence (the Death) which made such a profound impact on mediaeval religious feeling as retribution for sin. The "ryotoures" seated in the tavern are suddenly confronted in the midst of their ferocious lusts by an image of death.

> And as they satte, they herde a belle clinke
> Biforn a cors, was caried to his grave. C 665

Death was a person to the mediaeval mind, with its deep-rooted personifying impulse, and Death's victim is correspondingly seen as a sharp visual image.

> He was, pardee, an old felawe of youres;
> And sodeynly he was y-slayn to-night,
> For-dronke, as he sat on his bench up-right;
> Ther cam a privee theef, men clepeth Deeth,
> That in this contree al the people sleeth. C 676

In their drunken rage the rioters therefore rush forth to seek and to slay Death.

And we wol sleen this false traytour Deeth;
He shal be slayn, which that so many
        sleeth.   C 700

As they are about to cross a stile they do indeed meet someone who is equally anxious for death, an old man. . . . The huge power of the impression of that old man seems to proceed from the sense that he is more—or at least other—than a personal old man; that he possesses a non-human as well as a human force; that he seems "to recede from us into some more powerful life." [2] Though it is not said who he is, he has the original force of the allegorical Age (Elde). As Age he is connected with Death, comes as a warning of Death, knows about Death and where he is to be found.

To finde Deeth, turne up this croked wey,
For in that grove I lafte him . . .   C 762

("Croked wey" belongs to the traditional religious allegorical landscape.) The old man therefore knows more, is more powerful for all his apparent meekness and frailty than the proudest of the rioters who foolishly addresses him as an inferior and who may be supposed to shrink from the suggested exchange of his youth for the old man's age. The bare fact that we are impelled to wonder who or what the old man is—he is "al forwrapped"—produces the sense that he may be more than what he seems. He has been guessed (too easily) to be Death himself in disguise. Since that idea evidently occurs it may be accepted as an element of the meaning; but there is no confirmation, though he says that he wants to but cannot die and has business to go about. He has the terrible primitive simplicity—and therefore force—of an old peasant man whose conception of death is elementary and elemental.

And on the ground, which is my modres gate,
I knokke with my staf, bothe erly and late,
And seye, "leve moder, leet me
        in! . . ."   C 731

[2] Yeats, *Certain Noble Plays of Japan.*

When the rioters come to the tree to which the old man directs them they find not Death, a person, but a heap of bright new florins. We are thus brought round again to the theme of Avarice. The florins are the cause of their discord and several mutually inflicted deaths. The heap of florins turn out to have been indeed death in one of his diverse shapes. The recognition that Death is not after all a person, as we have been led to expect, and as the rioters as mediaeval folk had imagined, but that Death is more subtle, elusive and insidious—in this instance the deadly consequences of Avarice—comes as the last shock in the tale's succession of disturbing surprises.

Presuming his tale to have awakened in the company the full terrors of death and damnation, the Pardoner loses no time in producing his bulls and relics and offering them as a kind of insurance policy against accidents on the journey.

Peraventure ther may falle oon or two
Doun of his hors, and breke his nekke
        atwo.   C 936

He has the effrontery to call first upon the Host—"for he is most envoluped in sinne" —to kiss, for a small fee, his assoiling relics; but he quite loses his good humour when at last he gets the answer from the Host he has richly deserved.

Thou woldest make me kisse thyn old breech,
And swere it were a relik of a seint.   C 949

Yet even the Pardoner had deepened to a momentary sincerity (we cannot mistake it) when he said

And Jesu Crist, that is our soules leche,
So graunte yow his pardon to receyve;
For that is best; I wol yow nat deceyve. C 918

This final view of the queer teller of the tale sets it in a completed frame, as the peasant widow's poverty frames the tale of the brilliant Chauntecleer and makes a contrast between her sensible sobriety and his pretensions.

Charles A. Owen, Jr.

The Crucial Passages in Five of the *Canterbury Tales:*
A Study in Irony and Symbol

CHAUCER'S ART in the *Canterbury Tales* projects a complex world. To the dramatic pose of simplicity already adopted by Chaucer in many of his narrative poems is added the complication of a group of observed narrators. The intrinsic value of each of the tales is not its final one. Behind the artificial world created in the tale are the conscious purposes of the narrator and the self-revelation, involuntary and often unconscious, involved in all artistic effort. The simplest of the plots in the *Canterbury Tales* is that of the frame. It makes the same demand of each character involved, that he ride in the company of the others to Canterbury and back and participate in the creative activity of the tale-telling. Each character projects his tale, the limited vision it embodies, and his limiting personality into the world of the pilgrimage. The plot is simple but dynamic. For each vision has the potentiality of bringing into new focus those that preceded and of influencing those that will follow. The possibilities are soon unlimited. They lead to a richness that defies final analysis but finds its most concentrated expression in passages that at once embody and expose the limited vision of created character and creating narrator. These passages foreshadow in the unwitting speech or opinion of a character the outcome of the plot and help to create symbolic values that give the narrative an added and unifying dimension. They are in a sense symbolic of the whole work: in the contrast between what *is* and what men see—of

themselves and of others—lies Chaucer's deepest vein of comedy.

Passages that foreshadow the outcome in the unwitting speech of a character are fairly numerous in the *Canterbury Tales*,[1] but I have found only five that perform also a symbolic and unifying function. These five passages occur in five of the most important tales. It will be the purpose of this paper to analyze the five passages and to explore the multiple meanings, both within the tales and in the world of the pilgrimage, which they epitomize.

I

One of the clearest of the symbolic passages is the speech in the *Franklin's Tale*, where Dorigen softens her refusal to Aurelius and at the same time expresses her love for her husband:

But after that in pley thus seyde she:
"Aurelie," quod she, "by heighe God above,
Yet wolde I graunte you to been youre love,
Syn I yow se so pitously complayne,
Looke what day that endelong Britayne
Ye remoeve alle the rokkes, stoon by stoon,
That they ne lette ship ne boot to goon.

[1] Of special note are the two comments on learning by John the carpenter in the *Miller's Tale*, A 3449–64, and Symkin the miller in the *Reeve's Tale*, A 4120–26; and the twin laments at the end of Part I of the *Knight's Tale*, which set a pattern of parallel and paradox carried through to the end of the tale and thematically important. The lecture on anger that the Friar gives Thomas in the *Summoner's Tale*, D 1981–2092, lacks the concentration of the passages under discussion but performs the same functions.

Reprinted by permission from *JEGP*, LII (1953), 294–311.

I seye, whan ye han maad the coost so clene
Of rokkes that there nys no stoon ysene,
Thanne wol I love yow best of any man,
Have heer my trouthe, in al that evere I
     kan."   F 998

This speech of Dorigen provides the final element necessary to the plot. The happy marriage, the temporary absence of Arveragus, the enduring love of Aurelius, have all been presented. The wife's rash promise is the catalytic element that sets the others to reacting.

But because of the view we have had of Dorigen's grief, in which the rocks played so menacing a part, the rash promise is at the same time an expression of Dorigen's love for her husband. Her mention of the rocks tells us even more certainly than her refusal that she is entirely devoted to her husband. This speech introduces for the first time in the tale the contrast, extremely important later, between the appearance of things and the reality. On the surface the speech is an agreement under cetrain conditions to commit adultery. Beneath the surface it is an expression of conjugal loyalty.

In fact Dorigen has endeavored without realizing it to transform the symbolic meaning of the rocks. Up to this point they have represented to her the menace of natural forces to her husband's life. Hereafter their permanence is a guarantee of her enduring love for her husband. The rocks occur to her not only because her husband's life is in danger from them but because their immutability is like her love. She has seen beyond the menacing appearance of the rocks and has invoked the symbolic value of their endurance at the same time that she has finally accepted their reality.

The changed significance of the rocks is emphasized in several ways by Chaucer. Before her rash promise Dorigen questions on grounds of reason the purpose of the rocks in God's world and prays

"But wolde God that alle thise rokkes blake
Were sonken into helle for his sake!
Thise rokkes sleen myn herte for the
     feere."   F 893

After her promise to Aurelius it is his turn to pray for the removal of the rocks. Instead of Eterne God, he addresses Apollo, and asks him to persuade his sister Lucina to cause a two-year flood tide high enough to cover the rocks with five fathoms, or, if this is not feasible,

"Prey hire to synken every rok adoun
Into hir owene dirke regioun
Under the ground, ther Pluto dwelleth inne,
Or nevere mo shal I my lady wynne." F 1076

The parallelism of the prayers emphasizes the transformation of the symbol. The removal of the rocks is now the menace to the marriage. In both the prayers the desire to see the rocks removed is a sign of weakness, of unwillingness to accept the real world. Dorigen transcends her weakness when she accepts the permanence of the rocks. Aurelius transcends his weakness when he recognizes the quality of Dorigen's and Arveragus's love as superior to his own passion.

The rocks play an important part in the contrast between appearance and reality. There is never any question of doing away with the rocks: Aurelius's brother doesn't expect to achieve that when he proposes the trip to Orleans (F 1157 ff.), nor can the magican do more than make them *seem* to vanish.

But thurgh his magik, for a wyke or tweye,
It semed that alle the rokkes were
     aweye.   F 1296

Aurelius responds at first to the appearance of things.

he knew that ther was noon obstacle,
That voyded were thise rokkes
     everychon.   F 1301

But gradually he finds that the obstacles are still there. He himself makes no demand of Dorigen but merely reminds her of her promise. And when he hears of Arveragus's "gentillesse" and sees Dorigen's distress, he gallantly releases her. The real obstacles, like the rocks, only seem to have vanished. They are the honor, the decency, the gentility of all the people involved, and the true love of Dorigen and Arveragus for one another.

Dorigen's rash promise also functions in the tale in a way not intended by the Franklin. In addition to its other meanings it is an expression of "gentillesse" in its superficial sense. Dorigen tempers her absolute refusal in a way that makes it sound courteous, though in her heart she knows of the removal of the rocks,

"It is agayns the proces of nature."   F 1345

Even while accepting the natural order, she is shirking a part of her duty in the moral. That the rocks play so great a part in the thought and fate of this soft-hearted woman is a further irony. When faced at the end with the disappearance of the rocks and the necessity of keeping her promise, she will propose to herself suicide but allow her purpose to disintegrate as she calls to mind the sad fate of women who firmly carried out such a purpose.[2] Arveragus alone displays a firmness to which the rocks have relevance. His temporary absence makes possible the rash promise and his decision at the crisis forces Aurelius to see the "obstacles" that have only seemed to vanish. The superficial gentility of Dorigen's promise foreshadows and contrasts with the gentility of the ending, and the tale becomes a criticism of some aspects of gentility, more subtle than the Host's in the prologue to the tale (F 695), and more justified.

The Franklin presents in his tale an ideal of marriage and of "gentillesse," and manages at the same time to compliment the Knight, the Squire, and the Clerk. But his story is, without his realizing it, a critique of "gentillesse," for it is Dorigen's courteous softening of her refusal that makes the exhibition of gentility at the end necessary. The rocks which suggest the enduring value of gentility also suggest the distinc-

tions which the Franklin in his easy acceptance of the good things of life fails to make.

II

The crucial passage in the *Merchant's Tale* [3] comes in the middle of the epithalamion and sends echoes and reverberations through the two consultations and the marriage to a crowning climax in the garden scene at the end. The Merchant is showing us January's reasons for wanting to marry:

Mariage is a ful greet sacrement.
He which that hath no wyf, I holde him shent;
He lyveth helplees and al desolat,—
I speke of folk in seculer estaat.
And herke why, I sey nat this for noght,
That womman is for mannes helpe ywroght.
The hye God, whan he hadde Adam maked,
And saugh him al allone, bely-naked,
God of his grete goodnesse seyde than,
"Lat us now make an helpe unto this man
Lyk to hymself"; and thanne he made him Eve.
Heere may ye se, and heerby may ye preve,
That wyf is mannes helpe, and his confort,
His paradys terrestre, and his disport.
So buxom and so vertuous is she
They moste nedes lyve in unitee.
O flessh they been, and o flessh, as I gesse
Hath but oon herte, in wele and in
    distresse.   E 1336

The concept of marriage as an earthly paradise [4] has come to January late but with the blinding light of revelation: it has taken complete possession of his mind. The cautious habits and the short-sighted shrewdness of old age will be called on to support rather than examine his new vision. As in his judicious exclusion of the clergy and his appeal to example, he will use the forms of wisdom but not its substance. Marriage will carry all before it because it promises to combine the self-indulgence he has practised all his life with two things that old age makes vital to him for the first time—

[2] See James Sledd, "Dorigen's Complaint," *MP*, XLV (1947), 36 ff.

[3] In this analysis I am indebted to G. G. Sedgewick, "Structure of the *Merchant's Tale*," *UTQ*, XVII (1947–48), 337 ff.

[4] First stated at the beginning of the tale, E 1258–65, in a passage that adumbrates the one under discussion.

help for his physical weakness and the salvation of his soul. His lust for pleasure and his desire for salvation combine in the first consultation scene to blind him to the danger inherent in taking a young wife. The only danger he can foresee by the time he has chosen the girl and called his friends together the second time is so much felicity in marriage as to ruin his chance of a blissful after-life.

Besides epitomizing the precise and willful blindness of his attitude toward marriage, the passage foreshadows many of the details of his fate. The helpfulness that he anticipates in a wife will serve May as excuse for being in Damian's arms in the pear tree, and it will take the form before his very eyes of a nakedness similar to Adam's, her smock upon her breast (2395). But as he sees in Adam's story a proof of marital bliss, so he will see in the pear tree only what his wife wants him to, an example of her care for his welfare. The "unitee" and "o flessh" receive an ironical fulfillment in the blind old man's constant clutch on his buxom and perforce virtuous May, and an additional twist in the line from his invitation to the garden,

"No spot of thee ne knew I al my lyf," E 2146

where the irony of the contrast between his ugly passion and the romantic imagery and sacred associations of the Song of Songs (which is Solomon's!) matches the irony of his being as unconscious of the physical spot he is even then touching as he will later be of the moral spot—adultery—when he is looking at it with miraculously unblinded eyes.

The controlling images in the poem, however, are the linked ones of the garden, the blindness, and the tree. They are linked for the first time in this passage. "Heere may ye se," says the Merchant for January. But you can see in the story of Adam and Eve that a wife is man's earthly paradise, only if you are blind to the tree of the knowledge of good and evil and the forbidden fruit. As January is blind in the Garden of Eden,

so is he blind in the paradise (1822) of his wife's arms:

"A man may do no synne with his wyf,
Ne hurte hymselven with his owene
    knyf."   E 1840

Adam and Eve and the first sin link up in these fatuous lines with Damian,

Which carf biforn the knyght ful many a day
                                              E 1773

and the sin soon to be committed in January's private paradise. The garden that January builds is the consummation of his folly and the symbol of his marriage. Its beauty is May, and the stone wall with which it is "enclosed al aboute" is the jealous precautions of the blind January as well as the inescapable unpleasantness of his lovemaking. There is no stone of tyranny (1990) in May's nature, and in fact we find her pliancy which January expected to be like warm wax (1430) taking a ready impression (1978) from Damian's wooing. The silver key to the garden which is January's alone is his privilege as husband, but from the warm wax of May's nature a suitable replica is provided for Damian— his privilege as lover. The blindness is the physical counterpart of the ignorance of marriage and of women that January has shown all along. It prevents him to the end from seeing the tree in the garden and the knowledge of evil which it represents. And the regaining of his sight wipes out even the alertness to danger which accompanied the blindness.

The tree plays a further and more striking part in the tale. January fails to see it in the Garden of Eden, but brings it in as an image of his own virility in the first consultation with his friends:

"Though I be hoor, I fare as dooth a tree
That blosmeth er that fruyt ywoxen bee
And blosmy tree nys neither drye ne deed.
I feele me nowhere hoor but on myn heed;
Myn herte and alle my lymes been as grene
As laurer thurgh the yeer is for to
    sene."   E 1466

The image bears fruit in the final part of the story. In January's private paradise, his arms around the trunk of the pear tree, he serves his wife as stepping stone to the forbidden fruit of adultery. At the same time he becomes the symbol of his folly, cuckolded in the branches which spring from his head as horns.[5]

The imagery of growth has structural significance. The story is essentially the growth of an idea to complete fulfillment. Starting in the mind of January, a germ with all that develops already implicit, it attains in each part of the story a new mode of actualization—first verbal expression in general terms; then the fixing of the dream to a specific woman; then the literal fulfillment. At each stage January's blindness to his own folly achieves some new fatuity linked to the imagery in which he first clothed his "vision." [6] But the story does not stop with a single literal fulfillment. Through Proserpina's vow it suggests repetition through the ages. And it creates in the literal world the symbolic fulfillment of the idea. The garden and the blindness, in January's mind from the beginning, are now fully materialized. No miracle can make him see the tree as horns growing from his head, nor make him see the adultery committed before his very eyes.

The Merchant has taken care to tell us that this tale is not autobiographical:

"of myn owene soore,
For soory herte, I telle may namoore." E 1244

Moved by the ironical moral of the *Clerk's Tale*, he will join the discussion opened by

the Wyf of Bath and present directly a male view of marriage. The Wife and her theories are clearly in his mind for he commits the anachronism of having Justinus refer to her in the tale. His real intentions in telling the story are clear from two passages. In the prologue he says,

"We wedded men lyven in sorwe and care. . . .
                                          E 1228
As for the moore part, I say nat alle," 1231

And in the tale itself, speaking of Argus,

Yet was he blent, and, God woot, so been mo,
That wenen wisly that it be nat so.
Passe over is an ese, I sey namoore. E 2115

For the Merchant January is the type of that *rara avis*—the happily married man: Not all married men are miserable; some are blind.

The Merchant participates in the blindness of his creature January in not realizing the extent to which he is talking of his own sore in the tale. His imperceptiveness extends even to thinking that he can disguise the vulgarity of his tale in circumlocution. The circumlocutions in fact call attention to the vulgarity,[7] just as January's blissful ignorance contrasts with but does not conceal the Merchant's disillusionment. The creator of January is evidently a converted idealist, and the bitterness of his cynicism is the measure of his former folly. He can be so penetrating in exposing January's reasons for marriage because he is really looking at his own from beyond the gulf of two shattering months of marital experience. The cynical egoist looks at the delusions of an idealistic egoist and cannot see that his bitterness betrays him.

III

The *Wife of Bath's Tale* is ostensibly a two-part exposition of the Wife's thesis that marriages are happy only when the woman is the master. The crucial passage occurs when the "olde wyf" at the juncture of the

---

[5] The *OED* gives 1430–40 as the first instance of the cuckold's horns in English, but Robinson suggests a possible reference to them in the *Miller's Prologue*, A 3161, and the notion was certainly current on the continent. See, for instance, Boccaccio's *Decameron*, 5th Story, 7th Day.

[6] In the first consultation with January's friends there is the tree-virility passage already quoted. In the second consultation there is the fear "That I shal have myn hevene in erthe heere," E 1647. And in the marriage section there is the passage already quoted about sin and knives.

[7] For instance in E 1950 f., 1961 f., and 2361–63.

two parts reiterates in stronger terms her demand that the knight marry her:

"Nay thanne," quod she, "I shrewe us bothe
  two!
For though that I be foul, and oold, and poore,
I nolde for al the metal, ne for oore,
That under erthe is grave, or lith above,
But if thy wyf I were, and eek thy
  love."   D 1066

The old woman's demand is not only the conclusion of the quest plot, the price the knight pays for his life, but it is also the point of departure for the husband's dilemma. The woman must first secure her man before she can offer him her alternatives. The Wife of Bath's story passes with this speech from its public to its private demonstration of the thesis. The world-wide scene of the quest dwindles to the marriage-bed of the dilemma. We pass from generally accepted theory to the practice of one woman in achieving first sovereignty then happiness in her marriage.

But the husband's dilemma and the Wife of Bath's thesis are merely the surface of the story. The old woman has already demanded that the knight marry her. In her reiteration she reveals her real desire. She wants not just a husband but a husband's love. The phrase "and eek thy love" brought here into conjunction with the woman's ugliness, age, and poverty suggests that the real dilemma in the second part of the story is the wife's rather than the husband's; it foreshadows the necessity for miracle at the end and reveals for the story a second and more valid theme, operating on the instinctive level beneath the Wife's and her heroine's theories—the quest for love.

On this level the tale as a whole progresses from rape to marriage to love with each of the three crises of the story presenting a common pattern. In each there is a problem, a theoretical solution, and a modification of theory in practice. At the beginning of the story the knight's crime of rape is to be punished by death until the ladies intervene and send him off in quest

of crucial information about women. The second problem, what women most desire, is solved theoretically by the answer the knight gives the court. But it is clear from the "olde wyf's" demand that in practice one woman wants not sovereignty over husband and lover, but merely a husband and his love. The final problem is the obtaining of the husband's love, theoretically solved when he leaves the choice in his dilemma and thus the sovereignty to his wife. Actually the wife attains the knight's love by magically slipping between the horns of the dilemma and giving him exactly what he wants. The happy married life that results differs markedly from the blueprint of the Wife's thesis:

And she obeyed hym in every thyng
That myghte doon hym plesance or
  likyng.   D 1256

The Wife of Bath had good reason to tell the story she did. It provided what she considered a good demonstration of her theory. It gave her an opportunity of discussing a number of the questions close to her heart such as the true meaning of "gentillesse," and of parodying Arthurian romance with its unrealistic notions of life and love. It had the further appeal of an imaginative wish-fulfillment, for it presented an old woman who gained a young husband and magically changed herself into everything he could desire in a wife. As a story of the quest for love it was the artistic counterpart of her life.

In its continuing contrast between theory and practice the tale repeats the unconscious revelation of the Wife's prologue. For her theory of marriage and her own practice have been worlds apart. In her first three marriages she did maintain her sovereignty, but the marriages were not happy. No doubt the Wife enjoyed the cowed submission she so cleverly exacted from her old dotards. But she is forced to admit,

And yet in bacon hadde I nevere delit.   D 418

The fourth husband with his paramour aroused her jealousy and, to her satisfaction, became jealous in his turn. The Wife of Bath took refuge in travel, and the marriage was little more than nominal. Only with the fifth, her clerk of Oxenford, did she find happiness. Jankyn she cannot name without a blessing. But in the fifth marriage the relationship of the first three was simply reversed. This time she was twice his age and forced to sign over her property before the ceremony. Like the old woman in her tale she had to win his love. At the same time, she would have us believe, she won the upper hand in the marriage. That the triumph, like that of the heroine in her tale, is nominal her own words confess:

> After that day we hadden never debaat.
> God helpe me so, I was to him as kynde
> As any wyf from Denmark unto Ynde,
> And also trewe, and so was he to me.   D 825

We have further proof of the clerk's influence over her in the stress she puts on authorities in her discussions, in the clear memory she has for the stories in the book she made him burn, and in the strange distortion she makes of the Midas story in her tale. Jankyn left his mark on more than her "ribbes," more than her hearing.

The Wife of Bath enjoyed theory on one level and life on another. Her enjoyment of both was intense and convincing, so much so that most critics and readers have appreciated her gusto without noticing the contrast between her theory and practice in both prologue and tale.

IV

In the *Pardoner's Tale* [8] the crucial passage occurs at the point where the revelers find the pile of gold under the tree:

> No lenger thanne after Deeth they soughte.
>   C 772

[8] I am indebted in this analysis to Curry, *Chaucer and the Medieval Sciences*, 54 ff., and G. G. Sedgewick, "The Progress of Chaucer's Pardoner, 1880–1940," *MLQ*, I (1940), 431 ff.

On the primary level of the revelers' limited vision the wealth has driven all thought of their search for Death from their minds. They now think of the pleasures the gold will buy them and plan how to get it home safely. At the same time the statement foreshadows their end. They no longer seek Death because they have found him.

The single line marks a fundamental division in the tale. On the one hand is the drunken search for Death, marked by an unwonted and a deluded altruism. They are sworn brothers. They will slay Death. Drink has given them a mission, stature, pride, contempt for others. The gold has both a sobering and a deflating effect. It brings them back to the real world from their illusions of brotherhood and of slaying Death. Yet their drunken intentions were closer to the final outcome than their sober planning and counter-planning to secure the treasure. The gold has brought them back to their narrow world. It both focuses and limits their vision. These two sections of the tale, as we shall see later, have a symbolic value for the Pardoner.

But first we must explore the complex set of meanings in the tale as a whole. What happens to the gold in the story happens to the story itself. Its value is determined by the human motives focused upon it. In itself it may be an effective warning against cupidity, showing how greed turns gold into death. But as a part of the sermon habitually delivered by the Pardoner to the "lewed peple" it is at the same time the instrument of the Pardoner's greed. And as a part of the confession made to the other pilgrims it is the expression of the Pardoner's vanity. The pilgrimage gives him the opportunity to display to an intelligent audience the full measure of his cleverness and cynicism. He hopes so to dazzle and shock them that they will fail to see the motive that drives him to the compensation of hypocrisy and greed.

The Pardoner's physical disability has isolated him from some of the normal satisfactions in life. In revenge he has rejected the professed morality of other people and uses it against them to attain the power and comfort that wealth brings. His income is thus a symbol of his victory over physical inadequacy and of his superiority over the normal and stupid louts who are his victims. But the victory is not one that he can fully reveal in his daily life. Here, before the pilgrims, stimulated by the intelligence of his audience and with neither the necessity nor the possibility of assuming his customary role, he can for once reveal the extent of his success, impress his companions with the amount of his income, and shock them with the cynicism that makes it all possible. He seeks at the same time to conceal the emptiness and isolation of his life by reference to the comforts and gaieties he enjoys:

> "I wol have moneie, wolle, chese, and
> whete. . . .   C 448
> Nay, I wol drynke licour of the vyne,
> And have a joly wenche in every toun."   C 453

The task he has set himself in his confession is as wild and deluded as the drunken revelers' quest in the first part of the tale. Like the quest it has a wider range than his customary hypocrisy and is nearer the ultimate truth. But hypocrisy is his normal and sober world, and like the revelers' vision in the second part of the tale it is narrow and limited. The presumption of the pilgrim and the hypocrisy of the "noble ecclesiaste" both end in isolation. The Pardoner has also found death without recognizing it. His life is an exemplum of the futility of cynicism. And in the world of the pilgrimage, where we see the Pardoner but he cannot see himself, the crucial passage again functions.

v

The crucial passage in the *Nun's Priest's Tale* [9] is not so obviously a foreshadowing of the plot as in the other instances. It comes at the juncture between the discussion of dreams and the action of the near-

[9] I am indebted in this analysis to J. B. Severs, "Chaucer's Originality in the *Nun's Priest's Tale*," *SP*, XLIII (1946), 22 ff.

fatal third of May. Chauntecleer is speaking:

> "Now let us speke of myrthe, and stynte al this.
> Madame Pertelote, so have I blis,
> Of o thyng God hath sent me large grace;
> For whan I se the beautee of youre face,
> Ye been so scarlet reed aboute youre yen,
> It maketh al my drede for to dyen;
> For al so siker as *In principio*,
> *Mulier est hominis confusio*—
> Madame, the sentence of this Latyn is,
> 'Womman is mannes joye and al his blis.'
> For whan I feel a-nyght your softe syde,
> Al be it that I may nat on yow ryde,
> For that oure perche is maad so narwe, allas!
> I am so ful of joye and of solas,
> That I diffye bothe sweven and dreem."   B 4361

Here the ultimate victim employs the same technique in his deception of his wife as is later to be used by the fox on him—deceitful flattery. Behind the fair words of his translation, designed to smooth the ruffled feathers of Pertelote, whose laxatives have just been scorned, lurks the malicious dig of the Latin. The cock will later be "hoist with his own petard,"

> As man that koude his traysoun nat espie
> So was he ravysshed with his flaterie.   B 4514

Furthermore the cock is delighted with the sound of his own voice. In the long discourse on dreams, of which this is the conclusion, he has displayed the smug assurance of the born raconteur. And it is a moot point here whether his wife's beauty or his own cleverly barbed praise of it most attracts him. The cock is indeed ready to believe that other people admire his voice.

This speech of Chauntecleer brings out the pedantry implicit from the beginning in his actions. He alone can witness and appreciate the victory he has won over his wife. The victory is a pedant's triumph and contrasts strikingly with the one the fox later wins over him, which calls forth a universal clamor.

The cock's vast learning has furthermore contributed to the easy fatalism he has fallen into as a result of his learned rebuttal on dreams. The original dream was clearly a warning dream. The beast in it, which with all his learning the cock can describe but cannot recognize as his natural enemy the fox,

> "wolde han maad areest
> Upon my body, and wolde han had me
> deed."   B 4091

But in the examples which he uses to refute his wife's skepticism people either fail to heed the warning or they have no chance of evading the fate foretold in their dreams. The cock in effect wins the argument and forgets the dream that occasioned it. His pedantry has led him into a smug fatalism that contemplates his own coming "adversitee" (B 4341–43) as merely the concluding proof of the truth of dreams. No effort is called for—only the pursuit of what the soon-to-be-shipwrecked victim in one of the dreams called "my thynges" and the assumption of the courageous pose which Pertelote recommended and which his prowess makes ridiculous.

The cock, warned by dream and instinct against the fox and prepared by his own deft use of flattery against the technique the fox is to use, unwittingly gives himself a further warning, which he is either not learned enough or too pedantic to apply. Just as truly as the words of St. John's Gospel, woman is man's confusion, he tells his wife in Latin. But the words from the Gospel are *In principio*, in the beginning; and in the beginning Eve was Adam's confusion. So far is he from heeding the warning that the passage which contains it is full of the uxorious passion usually attributed to Adam. The cock's appreciation of his wife's charms diverts him from further thought of his own danger. Here in effect is another Adam, succumbing to the attractions of his wife when he should be using his reason. The Adam-and-Eve parallel, thus suggested for the cock-and-hen story, contributes to the mock heroics.

The passage is rich in other contributions to the mock heroic effect. It unites the language of exalted human passion with details of hen anatomy and barnyard architecture. The exalted language and the deflating details give the passage a quality that is typical of the whole poem. The courtly behavior and refined pretensions of Chauntecleer are constantly betrayed by the ludicrous activities and ignoble motives contingent upon chicken nature. The suggestion is clear: Objectively viewed, human pride and vanity are similarly betrayed. Only the simple life with frank acceptance of the necessities and limitations of the human lot, as exemplified by the widow and her menage, can have real dignity.

The contrast between Chauntecleer and his owner has a dramatic value in the *Canterbury Tales*. The Host in calling on the Prioress a little earlier addressed her in terms of the most exaggerated respect. Her Priest, however, he addresses with peremptory intimacy, making game of his poverty. When we remember the Prioress's pains

> to countrefete cheere
> Of court, and to been estatlich of manere,
> And to ben holden digne of reverence,   A 141

we can glimpse a guarded purpose. The sexes of the characters in the tale are reversed, as is also the ownership, but the essential relationship between poverty and wealth, between simplicity and pretension is there. The drama is carried a step further when the Priest falls into overt criticism of women (B 4442–49). This he does at the expense of the complexity of his tale. The advice of his wife is, as we have seen, a minor detail in the cock's decision. But it is a theme that the Priest attacks with evident relish. He brings himself up sharp with the thought of whom he might be offending, then returns to the attack indirectly by referring his listeners to the "auctors," and finally tries to ascribe the whole thing to the cock:

> "Thise ben the cokkes wordes, and nat myne;
> I kan noon harm of no womman
> divyne."   B 4456

The inner conflict of the misogynist employed by a woman has come for a moment to the surface; then it is pushed back behind the artifice of the story, where it has been operating secretly all along. The Host's reaction to the story has thus a double irony. Not only has he failed to see the point, but he imagines the Priest, if he were only a layman, a prodigious treader of hens!

The pedantry, ridiculed in the portrait of Chauntecleer, is also attacked by the Nun's Priest in his criticism of the rhetoricians. The satire is most highly comic when Friday and Master Gaufred are brought in at the climax of the story, and Venus is reproached for not protecting her devotee on her day, when it was her influence that was partly responsible for Chauntecleer's plight. It is possible, however, to ridicule a thing and be guilty of it on occasion oneself. This trap the Nun's Priest falls into at least once when he gets himself involved in a discussion of free will and God's foreknowledge—as a result of elaborating too far on a mock heroic color, (B 4420–40). Like Chauntecleer he is for a moment hoist with his own petard. And in struggling to get back to his tale, he suddenly finds himself involved in the criticism of women. Pedantry which leads to a criticism of women recalls the crucial passage and the cock's gibe, "*In principio,/Mulier est hominis confusio.*" The Priest in fact makes the same charge:

> Wommanes conseil broghte us first to wo,
> And made Adam fro Paradys to go,
> Ther as he was ful myrie and wel at
> ese.   B 4449

Whatever the cause for the Priest's misogyny (it may well be a combination of intellectual contempt and involuntary attraction), there is no mistaking the animus with which he follows his hero's lead in attributing man's ills to woman. This blanket condemnation of women is a very different thing from his implied criticism of the Prioress's pretensions. In his better moments he knows, as his portrait of Chauntecleer indicates, the real significance of Adam and Eve for mankind. *Hominis confusio* is man's own frailty. That the Priest lashes out at women as his stupid cock had done measures the strength of his feelings. In a sense these *are* the cock's words, and the Priest's recognition of their unworthiness enables him to recover his composure and his story.

On the primary level then the *Nun's Priest's Tale* is a brilliant and complex exposure of vanity, self-esteem, and self-indulgence through the mock heroic treatment of a beast fable. On the secondary level, the Nun's Priest joins the discussions of the Pilgrims on poverty (Man of Law and Wife of Bath), women's advice (Merchant), rhetoric (Host and Squire), and marriage. He is also presenting in the contrast between the widow and Chauntecleer a veiled comment on his position vis-à-vis the Prioress. Finally, on the level of involuntary revelation, he falls into the pedantry that he is ridiculing and uncovers for a moment in his confusion the feelings of a misogynist dependent on a woman. In this moment there is revealed a second conflict, the conflict between the artist, building with the materials of his art a world where his feelings achieve symbolic and universal expression, and the man, expressing his feelings directly.

CONCLUSION

The symbols which Chaucer employed are unobtrusive; they fit in their contexts of sentimental romance or crude realism without "shake or bind." Nothing in the tale forces them to the symbolic level. Yet the consistency with which the rocks are developed in the *Franklin's Tale* gives the obvious charm of the story a focused integrity which can be felt even when not clearly analyzed. The linked images of garden, tree, and blindness of the *Merchant's Tale* add to the bitter unity of tone an underlying unity of action: the seed of

January's folly grows from the fertile soil of his figurative blindness into the successive realizations of word, fixed purpose, and deed, until it attains full maturity in the garden, the blindness, and the tree-born fruit of adultery, with the head that canceived realistically behorned.

The focus and additional dimension which symbol and image provide in the tales are also attained by the contrast or ambiguity of the narrative elements involved. The intentional pattern of the *Wife of Bath's Tale* and the zest with which she tells it lose none of their literal value when we see the ambiguity of the elements she uses to prove her thesis. The nature of love and marriage resists the warping efforts of her dogged feminism and provides the counterpoint of a contrasting and more valid pattern. The quest for love which dominated her life dominates her tale. The greed in which the Pardoner has taken refuge creates the skillful weapon of his tale. With one edge he cynically dupes peasants; with the other he seeks to shock the pilgrims into a recognition of his importance. For the deluded vanity of the second purpose as well as the hypocrisy of the first, the two parts of his tale present analogies; at the very center the symbol of gold as unrecognized death reveals the futile emptiness of both efforts. The concealed purpose of the Nun's Priest finds urbane expression in the contrast between the simple dignity of the people and the ostentation of the chickens in his tale. But a momentary lapse into the pedantry he is mocking in Chauntecleer confuses him and he breaks through the artifice of beast fable to direct expression of his purpose. The artistic expression, where *hominis confusio* is man's own foolish presumption, forms an ironic background for the priest's lapse into an indiscriminate and direct antifeminism.

Chaucer, unlike the Nun's Priest, never expresses his intention directly. Present himself on the pilgrimage and in the occasional asides to the audience, he pictures himself as the simple reporter of experience, not responsible because unable to judge the questions of morals and propriety raised by the tales. Only in his own experience as narrator does the mask become penetrable, and then not to the pilgrims, his imaginary audience, who acquiesce in the Host's misunderstanding and crude estimate of *Sir Thopas* and get for their reward the prosy and long-winded idealism of the *Melibeus*. There is implied in the episode, as in the Man of Law's wrongheaded praise while cudgeling his brains for a tale, a comment on the popular taste and on Chaucer's relation to his real audience. Chaucer did not expect to be understood fully by all his readers. Certain of his effects depend on a knowledge which few of them could have. Others, like the crucial passages that have just been analyzed, are the subtle elaborations by the artist of a design already present. They suggest a personal standard and private satisfaction in his art.

But the simplicity adopted as a mask in the tales is not entirely ironical. It is a token for the deeper simplicity that receives impressions freely and refuses to interpose the eager evaluations, artistic and moral, that prevent full recognition. This deeper simplicity reflects faithfully the paradoxes of personality, the contradictions of experience. It becomes through its forbearance a rare and delicate instrument for evaluation and judgment, and presents a total vision not to be fully appreciated from the mental and spiritual posture of the Host, nor from that of the *homme moyen du moyen âge*, whom Chaucer could not only entertain but also see beyond.

Milton Miller

Definition by Comparison: Chaucer and Lawrence

I

CHAUCER'S NEGATIVE INCLUSIVENESS

IN *The Study of Poetry* Matthew Arnold tried to give Chaucer his due, and his criticism that Chaucer lacks the quality of high seriousness, as he called it, or of sublimity, as others have called it, may not be unwarranted. But it is not sufficiently qualified. For seriousness of some sort cannot be denied Chaucer. No reader of *Troilus* or the *Book of the Duchess* or the "Ballad of Good Counsel" ("Truth") can feel that he lacks either seriousness or insight of a very high order. Yet it is true that he seems almost to insist on avoiding that particular kind of seriousness Arnold calls high. The often quoted lines from the *Knight's Tale* seem almost to touch it (all Chaucer quotations are from F. N. Robinson's edition of *The Complete Works*):

> Now with his love, now in his colde grave
> Allone, withouten any compaignye.   A 2778

Yet when we read of Nicholas, in so different a setting in the *Miller's Tale*, that

> A chambre hadde he in that hostelrye
> Allone, withouten any compaignye,   A 3204

the repetition seems to parody the first use of the line, especially when we remember that it may well be by design, the *Miller's Tale* immediately following the *Knight's Tale* as it does. Or again, the ironic use he makes of the line "Lo, pitee renneth soone in gentil herte!" in the *Merchant's Tale;* a line he uses almost identically elsewhere with such different and such moving effect.

Arnold himself chose to compare him with Villon and particularly with the last stanza of Villon's "La Belle Heaulmière," to exemplify the high seriousness Chaucer lacked.

> Ainsi le bon temps regretons
> Entre nous, pauvres vieilles sottes,
> Assises bas, à croppetons,
> Tout en ung tas commes pelottes;
> A petit feu de chenevottes
> Tost allumées, tost estainctes.
> Et jadis fusmes si mignottes!
> Ainsi en prend à maintz et maintes.

If we cast about for something in Chaucer to compare with it, we discover that perhaps the closest parallel is to be found in the Wife of Bath, who says,

> But age, allas! that al wole envenyme,
> Hath me biraft my beautee and my pith.
> Lat go, farewel! the devel go therwith!
> The flour is goon, ther is namoore to telle;
> The bren, as I best kan, now moste I selle;
> But yet to be right myrie wol I fonde.   D 479

There surely is a sense in which the Wife might have been as pitiable as la belle Heaulmière, but it was not what Chaucer insisted on though he had the opportunity. Or, for one final example, since it too is reminiscent of Villon, no one who knows Villon's "Mais où sont les neiges d'antan?" will fail to feel the shock of recognition in "Ye, fare wel al the snow of ferne yere!" But apart from the very different effect Chaucer gets from the line in the mouth of Pandarus, the form of expression itself makes all the difference, even without the

Reprinted by permission from *Essays in Criticism*, III (1953), 369–377. This selection comprises the first two sections of an essay entitled "Definition by Comparison: Chaucer, Lawrence and Joyce." The third section compares Chaucer's *Book of the Duchess* with Joyce's *The Dead*.

surrounding circumstances: *fare wel* instead of Villon's *où sont.*

Yet if Chaucer seems to scout Arnold's high seriousness, it is not because he misses the point, but rather because he takes it for granted. The genius of comedy, Socrates insists at the end of the *Symposium* to the only two listeners still awake to hear him, Agathon and Aristophanes, is the same as that of tragedy. There may be, that is, a seriousness which subsumes them both. But from a Christian point of view like Chaucer's there is also a seriousness beyond them both, a sense of the human situation in which one is consciously and wholly implicated beyond self-justification and which he at the same time accepts as his due and does not revolt against. These two elements in themselves actively qualify the Greek concept of comedy and tragedy and in fact almost obviate it. For the distinction comes to be no longer between tragedy and comedy, the implacable and the ridiculous, but between humility and "folly." [1] For the author's degree of consciousness of the implication of himself, as well as his characters, qualifies the implacable and the ridiculous both by the introduction in the work itself of pity and love (charity, if you like); while acceptance of the old Adam, rather than revolt, permits no application of flattering unction to the soul. Tragedy is robbed of its tension, and it now deals with fortune not with fate. Though fortune in some sense replaces fate, it is not the same thing. Fate is implacable, high, wrathful, perhaps rather malignant. Fortune is pitiful, blind, untrustworthy, capricious. And the lack of consciousness of the extent of one's implication in the human (theological) situation becomes, if I may be permitted such a distinction, not a flaw but a "folly," that is, a sin. A similar situation in

[1] I am thinking of folly in the sense in which it is frequently used in the Old Testament, where it is coupled with iniquity or sin. For example, *Psalm* V. 5, "The foolish shall not stand in thy sight: thou hatest all workers of iniquity." Or *Proverbs* XXIV. 9, "The thought of foolishness is sin. . . ."

comedy is equally not simply ridiculous but "foolish," though it may be laughable and worthy of ridicule at the same time.

The tragic background of both the serious and the comic is of course the initial one of man's fall and his redemption; the joy of salvation involves the recollection of the passion, just as the passion itself involves the joyful issue of salvation. The distinction between the two is no longer an ethical but a religious or spiritual one involved in the idea of sin and grace. In that sense even Dante wrote not a tragedy but a "comedy." In the Middle Ages tragedy in the Greek sense is impossible, and what were called tragedies were merely set pieces illustrating the fickleness of fortune. Even *Troilus*, which might have been tragic, refuses the option. If Dante wrote one kind of "comedy," Chaucer wrote another, and the same seriousness underlies them both; but for both equally, conscious implication in the *condition humaine* and acceptance rather than revolt rule out, in the Greek sense, either tragedy or comedy.

Whether that is a loss need not concern us now; it is at all events a difference. And it gives us in Chaucer a world almost unfailingly affable, in which if one does not know the answer, one can *late it goon* because, of course, all the important things have been answered already. There is nowhere in Chaucer any unrelieved bitterness or harshness, such as one finds even in Shakespeare. But if Chaucer's world is affable, it is a world which never escapes a sense of its ultimate spiritual values; though folly may be delightful, among other things, yet it never escapes itself, it remains, like Dante's hell, a condition of the soul.

If Chaucer's wit is never bitter, that is because his world is in nothing perfect, exists in fact against an all-inclusive background of the impossibility of perfection. And Chaucer's world always included himself [2]—no dream of the perfect, whether an ideal of friendship or of conduct or of in-

[2] Sometimes, as in the *Canterbury Tales*, he even literally includes himself.

tellect could lead him to mistake himself even momentarily in his work for a transcendent creature whom an emotion of the unattainable exalts out of himself and his own humanity. Chaucer never attained the height of Dante's revelation, but he is not at variance with it. To paraphrase Lowell, he does for the world about us what Dante does for the world which is within us. Neither his subject nor his verse is Dante's, though so good a critic as Hazlitt in the lecture *On Chaucer and Spenser* was able to praise his verse, thinking particularly of the *Clerk's Tale* and the tale of the Prioress, for having "a religious sanctity about it." It has, he even goes on to add, "all the spirit of martyrdom."

To criticize Chaucer for lacking sublimity or high seriousness is then, when not further qualified, an objection taking only certain surface "positive" qualities into account and overlooking the deeper "negative" ones altogether. But after all the "negative" qualities turn out to be even more important than the "positive" ones. Where he may seem limited by the range or variety of what he actually did deal with, it is more meaningful to put it negatively and say that attitudes and qualities one takes for granted when he writes and never by implication denies in any considerable and varied body of literature covering a lifetime of creative activity, must surely be taken into the consideration of an author's inclusiveness. And in this sense Chaucer, though he may not be the most comprehensive and various, is nevertheless the least *ex*clusive of English writers. This gives him in fact a position of centrality from which not even the greatest of English writers displaces him. Chaucer is also, which is to put it another way, a way in which William Blake in his *Descriptive Catalogue* seemed to see it, the most typical of English writers.

And negatively too, since with Chaucer it is this negative one needs to insist on, his sublimity or high seriousness is apparent not by assertion but by his lack of confu-

sion of the sublime with the human. The less he asserts it, the more apparent it becomes as the regular habit of humility and of humanity which only a constant sense of the sublime or the serious could produce. For sublimity is not to be judged only by how far it is possible to rise or even how far it is possible to fall, but also by how far it is possible to stand without losing one's sense of distance either way; knowing, that is, where one stands in relation to the sublime. Chaucer, I am suggesting, has humility, and if that is not sublimity it is only another aspect of the same thing. That this relates Chaucer to Dante, for example, need hardly be insisted on, any more than the way it differentiates him from Dante. But one needs to stress the difference as much as the relation, for it is the difference which English literature follows; the relation is finally a relation to European literature as a whole.

One may miss in Chaucer, as Arnold does, the accent of such a verse as Dante's "In la sua voluntade è nostra pace." But that precise accent in Dante escapes English verse altogether. Neither "The rest is silence," nor "Ripeness is all" approaches it. Other "accents" which English poetry after him continues to echo Chaucer does get, like

> Us from visible and invisible foon
> Defende   *T. and C.* V, 1867

or

> But deeth, that wol nat suffre us dwellen heer,
> But as it were a twynklyng of an ye,
> Hem both hath slayn, and alle shul we
>   dye.   E 38

Chaucer, then, is limited in the range of what he actually has dealt with, but what he deals with does not comprehend the range of what he takes for granted and never, by implication, excludes. The quality of terror or of horror, for example, Chaucer does not particularly cultivate. Yet that too is not excluded however it may be softened, as it is in *Troilus*, for example, or in the *Pardoner's Tale,* in the Griselda story or in the *Franklin's Tale,* to take only the most random examples. Terror tempered by grace underlies Chaucer's world as the ever present possibility which, if it be kept far hence, may yet at any moment be dug up again.

> Us from visible and invisible foon
> Defende.

Chaucer is not simply summed up. His work is delicate, intricate, carefully and highly wrought. He sees life steadily, and if he is not omnilateral, he *is* manysided.

II

THE PRIMEVAL SOCIAL INSTINCT

Vitalism, which has been a central concern of modern literature, perhaps finds its most influential expression in the work of D. H. Lawrence. And the individual, social and sexual vitalism Lawrence sought is in many ways akin to the vitality Chaucer had. There is an opportunity for a direct comparison offered us in the coincidence that Lawrence's cock in *The Man Who Died,* so central a symbol in that story (Lawrence's own title for the story was "The Escaped Cock"), is in many ways similar to Chauntecleer who points a moral in the *Nun's Priest's Tale.*

Chauntecleer is a cock without frustrations, either social or sexual, who thoroughly accepts his world and does not try to escape it. He is indeed the norm of all cocks, whose descendant Lawrence's bird is. And certainly he is not less splendid than Lawrence's "saucy, flamboyant bird," his "black and orange cock with the red comb, his tail feathers streaming lustrous." More so perhaps:

> His coomb was redder than the fyn coral,
> And battailled as it were a castel wal;
> His byle was blak, and as the jet it shoon;
> Like asure were his legges and his toon;
> His nayles whitter than the lylye flour,
> And lyk the burned gold was his
> colour.   B 4054

Nor does he show less vitality; he is not less a cock, he is the essence of cock.

There is some similarity of intention as well as detail. They both stand out royally from their squalid surroundings, and for the same reason, what Lawrence calls their flaminess. In the magnificence of their crowing they "cry out the triumph of life." Lawrence's cock, however, cries out his triumph in a restless, ceaseless attempt to escape from social compulsion. And it is in spite of compulsion that he crows "triumph and assertion," imprisoned as he miserably is "by a cord of circumstance" to the barnyard from which he has once already tried to escape. Chauntecleer crows the triumph of a life he is and has been enjoying in a barnyard whose world he never thinks of escaping. In it

> . . . Chauntecleer so free
> Soong murier than the mermayde in the
> see.   B 4460

His crowing had no peer anywhere. It had, Chaucer says, a blissful sound and was more certain than the clock. "For whan degrees fiftene weren ascended," that is precisely on the hour, "Thanne crew he, that it myghte nat been amended." When Chauntecleer is finally carried out of his barnyard by the fox, it is against his will and only under compulsion: there is no greater calamity for him. For in his own barnyard with his seven hens Chauntecleer is "roial, as a prince is in his halle."

In order that Lawrence's magnificent cock may be thrown "into the seethe of phenomena" to "ride his wave," the man who died finally carries him to another barnyard, where, after conquering the reigning cock there, he is left to take up a new life. The change, meant to be a significant one, fails in many ways to be quite convincing and seems, from one point of view, a curiously futile one, from one barnyard to another merely. At all events, Chauntecleer seems to begin just at the point at which the cock in *The Man Who Died* ends. For in his own yard he already dwells in "the seethe of phenomena" and is there riding his wave magnificently indeed.

Lawrence says in a letter to the psychologist Dr. Trigant Burrow that the "primeval societal instinct" is "much deeper than the sex instinct" and its repression is "much more devastating." It is interesting, in this light, to notice that his cock escapes from constraint and compulsion into an *aloneness* that "can take on splendour, polished by the lure of [his] hens." Whatever difference the change is meant to have made, whatever the sexual polish and splendour, the very freedom of the cock, his escape from compulsion and his achievement of *aloneness*, itself precludes any real social fulfilment. We shall understand this better if we turn to Chauntecleer for comparison. Like Lawrence's cock he is "full of life and virtue," but his splendour is societal as well as sexual. His very fault, which gives a moral to the story, is a social one, he is amenable to flattery. *Aloneness* would have seemed no achievement; he would not have understood it, being debonair and socially easy, as cocks are. His life is not, in its uniqueness, a drag upon his pleasure in living; it is the condition of his pleasure, which he accepts. Not so his descendant, whose flaming life is a burden under the uniqueness of which he cannot rest in the impersonality and splendour of the social moment, but must seek a personal identification of himself beyond the moment. For the social moment is, as it is for the man who died himself, a merely "infinite whirl."

What after all the cock does not know, or what at least the man who died confuses, is that the "seethe of phenomena" is not *aloneness* but the life of society, and that the dread of compulsion is the dread of living a social life in a society which holds out no adequate spiritual end, frustration instead of fulfilment, where there is not only the greed of taking but "the greed of giving" as well. The man who died can see the life of society only as "a vast complexity of entanglements and allurements" from which he too seeks to escape. Chauntecleer does not know the same social frustration and so he does not have the same need to think his social fulfilment unique, involving a separate and personal spiritual identification with the source of life. He would have been amazed to hear his descendant described as having "risen to the Father, among birds." For the sons have in nothing surpassed the fathers, neither in crowing nor in treading. And where would be the point in sainting a cock for his cockishness? It is merely the condition of his being a cock at all.

Bertrand Bronson

Chaucer's Audience

THE QUESTION of the dynamic relationship of one story to another; the happy use of personal antagonisms among the pilgrims to generate attack and counterattack; the brilliant notion of a symposium upon a single theme: these are matters of absorbing interest that lie beyond the province of the present discussion, which is concerned with dramatic technique only as it is connected with, or grows out of, Chaucer's narrative technique in relation to his audience.

It is evident that the other side of the problems we have been considering is the nature and quality of that audience. If it be true that Chaucer kept in view, while he wrote, the needs and predilections of those who were to hear him, it is true also that, in a sense, his works are a judgment of his public. We have a right to deduce the character of that public, in a general way, from the indications of it that we find in his poetry.

Some of the things which Chaucer and, by natural inference, his audience take for granted, are shocking to a later age, which in particular directions has acquired greater refinement of feeling. No quality is more characteristic of Chaucer's own sensitive nature than compassion—

For pitee renneth soone in gentil herte.

Yet Chaucer accepts, as callously as a modern American police officer, certain barbarities of conduct connected with the administration of justice. When, for example, in the *Man of Law's Tale*, after a passage of inexpressible pathos, Constance has been set adrift upon the sea with her little son, Chaucer passes to the inquiry which King Alla instituted upon his return. The messenger who had been instrumental in this miscarriage was, it will be remembered, though obtuse and stupidly susceptible to the temptations of drink, entirely innocent of intentional wrongdoing. He is not merely questioned, however, about his actions. Chaucer describes what happened to him in the following matter-of-fact way:

This messager tormented was til he
Moste biknowe and tellen, plat and pleyn,
Fro nyght to nyght, in what place he had
    leyn.   B 887

Nobody, apparently, is troubled by the needless severity of this procedure, or regards it as other than a matter of course. Again, in the *Troilus*, the implications of the Polyphoetes episode—an invention of Chaucer's—are instructive in this connection. The assumption throughout is that the normal means of obtaining satisfaction in a dispute about land is not primarily recourse to due process of law, but the enlisting against one's opponent of as many as possible of the nobility, in order to forestall his success. It matters not that the present quarrel is a mere device of Pandarus to secure other ends. Deiphebus promises to be Criseyde's champion "with spere and yerde"; and Pandarus asserts that with his potent assistance and that of his brother, her adversaries are sure to be terror-stricken. Afterwards, at the dinner party arranged in Criseyde's interest, Pandarus

Reprinted from *Five Studies in Literature,* University of California Publications in English, Vol. 8, No. 1, University of California Press, 1940. This selection is Part VI of "Chaucer's Art in Relation to His Audience."

rong hem out a process lik a belle
Upon hire foo, that highte Poliphete,
So heynous, that men myghte on it spete.

Answerde of this ech werse of hem than other,
And Poliphete they gonnen thus to warien:
"Anhonged be swich oon, were he my brother!
And so he shal, for it ne may nought varien!"
What shold I lenger in this tale tarien?
Pleynliche, alle at ones, they hire highten
To ben hire helpe in al that evere they
    myghten.   *T. and C.* II, 1624

Once more, in the same connection, the brutality of the attitude toward the Jewish race expressed in the *Prioress's Tale* will occur to many readers.

The question of indecency in Chaucer's work is still more apparent than the unconscious injustices. In this matter, we need not attribute to the poet a special taste for the pornographic; and no sensible reader will accuse him of being primarily interested in this aspect of even his grossest tales. It is simply obvious that part, if not all, of his public tolerated a greater freedom of expression than is permitted in most companies today. Of smirking innuendo, however, there is singularly little to be found in Chaucer's work. Neither in the fabliaux nor in the links is there any noticeable tendency to hint the sly obscenity. It is his habit, in the main, and the habit of his characters, to be either blameless or frankly indecent. The few places where we can detect the leer are remarkable because they seem so out of key with the context. For example, in the delicate prologue to the *Legend of Good Women,* there is an offense of this kind. Speaking of the birds' delight in the springtime, the poet writes:

  therwithalle hire bekes gonnen meete,
Yeldyng honour and humble obeysaunces
To love, and diden hire other observaunces
That longeth unto love and to nature;
Construeth that as yow lyst, I do no
    cure.   *L. G. W.* F 152

It is noteworthy that Chaucer removed this blemish when he revised the prologue. There is a hint of sly indelicacy in the *Man*

of *Law's Tale;* [1] and possibly another in the *Knight's Tale.* [2] Also in the *Knight's Tale* occurs a jocular reference which strikes one as ill judged. [3] A similar note is struck once in the *Merchant's Tale:*

But lest that precious folk be with me wrooth,
How that he wroghte, I dar nat to yow telle;
Or wheither hire thoughte it paradys or
    helle;   E 1964

and the Merchant also indulges in a needless circumlocution, apparently for off-color effect, because only a few lines further on he uses the word now avoided. [4]

All the other instances of this kind of thing which have been noted occur in the Wife of Bath's prologue, where, indeed, they seem dramatically appropriate as being the characteristic habit of her mind. The Wife passes from the grossest and most outspoken terms and the frankest expression of her most intimate thoughts, to what would be called today a "nasty niceness," mincing her words for indecent effect. Contrast, for instance, her feigned decency in the following lines:

Ye knowe what this ensample may resemble;
                 D 90

and

Ye woot wel what I meene of this, pardee!
                 D 200

with the grossness of her expression elsewhere.

But the enjoyment of the frankly gross is commonly accompanied by a tolerance of innuendo; and it is remarkable that Chaucer has kept the two so distinct, and been so seldom guilty of the latter. On the few occasions where he has used it in the nondramatic poems, one may perhaps, since it seems to be foreign to his disposition, attribute the fault to the temptation of secur-

[1] B 708–714.
[2] A 2284–8.
[3] A 2388–90.
[4] E 1950–51.

ing a cheap reward from his audience. That the temptation was not more compelling may be set down partly to the credit of the fundamentally sound taste of that audience.

In one other matter, Chaucer and his audience sinned even more egregiously than English-speaking peoples today, though the current is moving in his direction. I refer to the use of oaths, which all Chaucer's characters employ, with impressive variety and copious profusion. "Benedicitee! What eyleth [hem] so synfully to swere?"

But when all due subtractions have been made, the audience which can be discerned from its reflected image in Chaucer's work must compel our admiration. Clearly they were far more highly civilized than the audience which Shakespeare and his contemporaries had to address. Sensitive in most things, quick to catch the refinements of the subtlest humor and the finest irony, they must have been perceptive to a degree seldom attained in our own day. They must, I say, have been so, because no poet could have gone on producing the highly socialized kind of poetry which is Chaucer's characteristic work, without the encouragement of a ready and immediate appreciation. Has an audience ever been given a finer testimonial of quality than that which is embodied in the gift of works so subtle, so various, so beautiful, as the *Parlement*, the *Franklin's Tale*, the *Nun's Priest's Tale*, the *Prioress's Tale?* Surely they deserve our gratitude, those men and women of Chaucer's circle; for it is partly owing to them that for us today Geoffrey Chaucer is the best company in the world.

Morton W. Bloomfield

Chaucer's Sense of History

"Die Geschichte der verschiedenen Arten des Sehens ist die Geschichte der Welt."

—EGON FRIEDELL, *Kulturgeschichte der Neuzeit.*

I

THE GROWTH of a sense of history from the twelfth century until our own time which has culminated in the various forms of historicism, empiricism, and cultural anthropology was nourished by the importance given to history by Christianity. And Christianity emphasizes the significance of history because it is based on revelation, wherein the timeless meets time and dignifies it. It believes that profound qualitative changes essential to human salvation have occurred and will occur in history.

It is a commonplace of the history of ideas that Israel gave the Western world a philosophy of history, just as Greece gave it a philosophy of nature. The Israelite philosophy of history was based on the idea that history has a transcendental meaning and is not just a repetitive cycle, that it reveals the will of God, that God may interfere and has interfered with the process of history, and that history is partially redemptive and moves towards a final end. Unlike the gods of Greece, the God of Israel Himself has no history; but again unlike the Greek concept of its own history, Israel and the other nations have a supremely significant history.

The ancient Hebrews saw, for instance, three main stages in which man's obligations and concepts differ—a time before the Law, the time after the Law, and a time to come under the Messiah before the final days and the end of all history. There is a movement forward, a *development* in history. Even the fact that the supreme revela-

tion to the Israelites was in the Law [1] gives a historic and social character to God's activity. These ideas are not, however, explicitly stated in the Bible and ancient Jewish tradition, but they are implicit in most of the strongly existentialistic writings of the Hebrew people.

Christianity took over these basic historic postulates and beliefs from Judaism and introduced another historic stage initiated by the Incarnation in which the Law is superseded by Grace. The Pauline conception of eras *ante legum, sub lege,* and *sub gratia* sums up this reinterpretation of history. But Christianity also looks forward to a Coming (a second one) of the Messiah in history. No one in the Judeo-Christian tradition can ignore history, and the claims of Christianity and Judaism as religions rest upon the historicity of certain happenings in the past. They stand or fall on the truth of these events. If no revelation in time on Mount Sinai, if no Christ, Son of God, who actually lived in Galilee and Judea some two thousand years ago, then no religions of Judaism and Christianity.

The Greek emphasis was, however, essentialistic, natural and metaphysical, not existentialistic, supra-natural and historic. And in its impact on the Christian and Jewish religions, it tended to develop a philosophy of religion, an essentialistic and metaphysical approach.[2] But even in St.

[1] The act of Creation was of course God's supreme revelation to all men; but to the Jews as such, the Law is God's highest revelation.

[2] See Martin Foss, *The Idea of Perfection in the Western World*, 1946, pp. 26 ff.

Reprinted by permission of author and editor from *JEGP*, LI (1952), 301–313.

Thomas, who more than any other Christian thinker applied the Greek categories to Christianity, the sense of the historic is not absent.

The Middle Ages generally, however, tended to ignore the implications of a historic sense on matters outside of religion. This was due in part to a lack of knowledge of other times and other cultures, and in part to an overwhelming emphasis on a few historic events of the highest religious significance. These events were often assimilated to an extra-historical reality. Christ is sacrificed every minute of the day, and man continually falls, as he did once in the long long ago. Every enactment of the Mass goes through the redemptive process all over again. By this hypostasizing of the extremely important events in the Christian story, the Middle Ages developed, in effect, an a-historic (not un-historic) approach which could—and did to some extent—blur the historic approach.

With the renaissance of the twelfth century, we find, as a result of the Crusades, new translations and other factors, the emergence of a new knowledge and a new methodology which made possible a new historic sense (or better a *Diesseitsstimmung* [3]). This may be seen in Biblical exegesis,[4] in Gothic art, in the popularity and number of histories and chronicles,[5] in new historical theorizing and millenarianism, observable for instance in the works associated with Joachim of Flora and some of his Franciscan followers,[6] in the revival of interest in the Classics, and in the variety and types of vernacular literature. In some ways Aristotelianism was a retarding force from this point of view, and it was not until Aristotle began to lose his hold on men's minds in the fourteenth and fifteenth centuries that the growth of the historic sense could have full play. Yet Christian Aristotelianism with its emphasis on natural reason left a strong imprint on some of the pre-suppositions and justifications of this sense of history.

What is meant by a historic sense in this new development? It is clearly not the basic historic postulates of Christianity, for they are the matrix of the new sense and were of course never superseded. It is rather basically a new heightened attention toward past, present and future. It may manifest itself in an emphasis on the pastness of the past or on the reality of the present or on a concrete hope or despair for the future. Only occasionally in its early phases, do we find in one person a three-fold emphasis, as in Chaucer, but usually it is manifested only in an awareness of one or two of the traditional divisions of time. In the Joachimite movement, the accent is on the future; in the new naturalism in art and literature it is implicitly on the present; and more rarely, in historians, a new awareness of the past is found. In sum, it is a *Diesseitsstimmung*—a this-world orientation which, however, did not deny the other world.

---

[3] There is unfortunately no good English equivalent for this German term. It is more accurate than the phrase " sense of history" which I have used in this paper.

[4] The twelfth and thirteenth centuries, in part due to the influence of the Jewish exegete Rashi, insisted more strongly on the literal (which was also known as the historical) level of interpretation than on the other allegorical (and more figurative) levels. This attitude also manifested itself in current attitudes towards literature; see Charles S. Singleton, "Dante's Allegory," *Speculum*, XXV (1950), 78–86.

[5] The twelfth century saw an efflorescence of historical writing, especially in England and Germany. See C. H. Haskins, *The Renaissance of the Twelfth Century*, 1927, pp. 224 ff.

[6] For works in English on medieval theories of history and the writing of history and related ideas, see George Boas, *Essays on Primitivism and Related Ideas in the Middle Ages*, 1948; and very generally in Chapter 1 of Ernest Lee Tuveson, *Millennium and Utopia, A Study in the Background of the Idea of Progress*, 1949. Erich Auerbach in *Mimesis* associates the rise of late medieval "realism" in subject-matter and style with the Franciscans and their emphasis on the life and sufferings of Jesus. See pp. 141 ff. in the Anchor edition of the English translation by Willard Trask.

Approaching the question from another angle, we may also say that the new historic sense is demonstrated in (1) a more accurate sense of chronology and (2) a sense of cultural diversity. Neither is new; both may be found in the early Fathers and in some of the Classical writers. But they waited upon knowledge and favorable circumstances to be fully applied to the processes of history. They also in some measure demand both a sceptical or at least open spirit and a conviction that the things of this world matter (or a partially secular point of view), for a pure interest in history would be considered merely another vanity by a Saint Bernard or by a Richard Rolle. They require the existence of intellectuals who will be concerned with the problems of this world and who will be willing to forgo at least temporarily, the proper end of man from the religious point of view —the union with, or vision of, God. Or more subtly, intellectuals who believe they are doing God's work by being concerned with the things of this world. Philosophically they also need the concept of an autonomous realm of reason and a concept of natural law, which the scholastics provided or at least presented in acceptable form.

How does Chaucer stand in relation to this idea of the idea of history? Or, what is his sense of history? How does a knowledge of Chaucer's sense of history help us to interpret his work? To these questions the remainder of this article will be devoted.

II

In his early work there is little evidence of a sense of history, but in *The Legend of Good Women, Troilus,* and the *Canterbury Tales*, we find an increasing preoccupation with both accurate chronology and cultural diversity and a strong feeling for the past, the present and the future. I shall take for granted an increasing naturalism in Chaucer's work, a movement away from allegory towards representationalism, which in itself is a manifestation of the sense of the historic as present. We also find in Chaucer's later works, an increasing tendency to date and to localize his narratives. As a source for his changed point of view, it is possible to look to the early Italian Renaissance of which Chaucer had first hand experience. But although rare, there are also, as we shall see, signs of an incipient sense of the historic in contemporary England.

Although in Chaucer we often find flagrant anachronisms, they usually arise out of ignorance, thoughtlessness, or the superior claims of artistic fitness. We may, if we wish, make up an impressive list of Chaucer's historical errors and falsifications, probably larger than the list which illustrates his sense of history. But that is not the point. What is remarkable is that Chaucer is historically minded as compared with his English contemporaries and that on the whole, in his later works, he has a considerable sense of historic succession and cultural relativity.

At least two of his characters apologize for violating chronology. In the *Knight's Tale*, describing the "Temple of myghty Mars the rede" the Knight tells us of the murals within the building, some of which dealt with future events (after the time of Theseus)—the murders of Julius Caesar, of Nero and of Caracalla (listed in proper chronological order). He goes on to say that although they were not born yet, their deaths were, nevertheless, depicted there (ll. 2031 ff.).[7] The mere prediction is standard astrology, but significant is Chaucer's qualifying phrase "al be that thilke tyme they were unborn. . . ." The Monk also apologizes before he tells his tragedies:

But first I yow biseeke in this mateere,
Though I by ordre telle nat thise thynges,
Be it of popes, emperours, of kynges,
After hir ages, as men writen fynde,
But tellen hem som bifore and som bihynde,

[7] Chaucer was very much interested and may have believed in some form of judicial astrology as did many of the learned men of his time. The idea that the future was written in the stars is clearly enunciated in the *Man of Law's Tale*, ll. 190 ff.

As it now comth unto my remembraunce,
Have me excused of my ignoraunce.   B 3180

In the "Legend of Lucrece" (ll. 1812 ff.), Chaucer uses his sense of the past to give an ironical twist to his comments pointing towards later times.

These Romeyn wyves lovede so here name
At thilke tyme, and dredde so the shame,
That, what for fer of sclaunder and drede
  of deth,
She [Lucrece] loste bothe at ones wit and
  breth. . . .

This passage is a particularly happy example of the marriage of Chaucer's sense of the past with his own sense of humor and satire, the first serving the second.

Some further passages in Chaucer provide evidence both of his sense of chronology and of his awareness of cultural differences. In the *Man of Law's Tale*, Constance, daughter of the Emperor of Rome, lands on the coast of Northumberland and properly speaks a Vulgar Latin to the inhabitants. As Robinson says, "Indeed the whole account of Roman Britain in the tale conforms to historic fact to a degree unusual in mediaeval stories." [8] Chaucer may well have been aware of the fact that in the time of a Roman Emperor the inhabitants of Britain would be speaking or would at least understand a "manner Latyn corrupt" (l. 518), even though his source had the inhabitants speaking Saxon. Or at least this passage shows that he was deliberately making the ancient Britons speak Latin instead of Saxon. At the same time, however, he seems blind to the fact that a Mohammedan Sultan could not have been ruling coevally in Syria, unless he is deliberately mixing up eras here for an artistic effect of make-believe. I suspect not, however, and think rather that we have in the *Man of Law's Tale* an unconscious blend of the medieval and modern senses of chronology.

Professor Tatlock has pointed out that Chaucer is deliberately archaizing the set-

ting of the *Franklin's Tale*. The *Tale* is made to unfold as in Roman times, and there is no suggestion for this in any imaginable source. We may see this archaism in the use of the term Armorica for Brittany, in allusions to heathens (l. 1293) and heathen gods (ll. 1030 ff.), in a reference to the worthlessness of certain aspects of natural magic "as in oure dayes is not worth a flye" (l. 1132), and possibly in the use of the ancient town of Kayrrud (l. 808). And yet we find in heathen days, a University at Orléans. Professor Tatlock suggests that "Chaucer put the whole tale back in pagan times that the Franklin might with the more propriety rail at such arts [astrological magic] as heathenish and might disavow serious approval of them, or faith in their efficacy, especially for an evil purpose." [9]

It is possible that this is the explanation, but I am inclined rather to think Chaucer's method here an attempt to throw an aura of the past over the fantastic happenings reported. One reason does not necessarily exclude the other, and in any case Chaucer shows here in his accumulation of details an intense awareness of the pastness of the past and the difference between those days and his own. He turned to the past in order to make his *Tale* palatable, and in so doing reveals an awareness of the problem of time and credibility.

So too for a humorous effect does the Wyf of Bath lament the passing of incubi and elves who used to infest the land and waylay women (ll. 857 ff.). She contrasts the unhappy present when there are only friars about to carry out this pleasant function, with the happy past. *Autres temps, autres mœurs*, alas! She also points out here how the Welshmen and Britons idealize their Arthurian history.

In the famous passage in *Troilus and Criseyde* II, 22–28, we read

[8] F. N. Robinson, *The Works of Geoffrey Chaucer*, second edition, 1957, p. 694.

[9] See John S. P. Tatlock, *The Scene of the Franklin's Tale Visited* (Chaucer Society, Second Series 51), 1914, p. 21.

Ye knowe ek that in forme of speche is chaunge
Withinne a thousand yeer, and wordes tho
That hadden pris, now wonder nyce and
    straunge
Us thinketh hem, and yet thei spake hem so,
And spedde as wel in love as men now do;
Ek for to wynnen love in sondry ages,
In sondry londes, sondry ben usages.

In this melancholy stanza on the passage of time, Chaucer reveals not only a sense of chronology but also an acute sense of cultural change in regard to the past and present. It is not merely a conventional comment on human transience, but a statement of the accumulative effect of time on human customs and manners. Here also is the medieval and Greek sense of a permanence underlying all change—the one behind the many.

A sense of historical development applying this time to the future is to be found at the end of *Troilus* (V, 1793 ff.) where Chaucer argues from the contemporary diversity of the English language and from the sound changes going on in his time to the conclusion that English may change so drastically in the future that some may miswrite, mismeter or misunderstand him. From both of these *Troilus* passages, we get a poignant sense of the inexorable quality of time. Chaucer tells us by implication that he himself will pass away along with all these other ephemera.

Shortly after (ll. 1835 ff.), he goes on to contrast the world before Christ with that after His death when He introduced a new kind of love to mankind, very different from that revealed in the story of Troilus and Criseyde which he has just been narrating. The world *sub gratia* is a very different world; a new quality or dimension has been created by God's love, dividing forever pagan history ("while men loved the lawe of kinde") from Christian history.

Even more common in Chaucer is a sense of cultural diversity between the past and the present. At least three times in the *Knight's Tale*, he explains, following Boccaccio from whom he possibly derived his

historic sense, the actions of his characters with the modifying clause, "as was tho the gyse" or a similar clause. The funeral customs of Thebes (l. 993), the sacrificial rites of Athens (l. 2279), and the Athenian cremation ceremonies (l. 2911) are so qualified. Similarly in "The Legend of Cleopatra" in *The Legend of Good Women* (ll. 583 ff.), we find Chaucer's comment "as was usance," on Anthony's being sent "for to conqueren regnes and honour/Unto the toun of Rome."

Chaucer's awareness of the difference in human custom also extends to those two coeval peoples, the Greeks and the Trojans. Diomede's light chatter to Criseyde in his campaign to win her, includes a solicitous inquiry "if that hire straunge thoughte/The Grekis gise, and werkes that they wroughte" (V, 860–61), A pleasant enough topic of conversation, but revealing in Chaucer a knowledge that not only are customs past and present different, but also that contemporary customs in the past may vary. And again Chaucer, for purposes of his humor, makes a mock and yet true distinction between ancient mythological figures and ancient Biblical figures of names similar enough to be frequently confused. In the *Knight's Tale* (ll. 2062 ff.) we are told that Dane (i.e. Daphne), not Diane, was turned into a tree. The Pardoner is also careful to tell us he is referring to Lamuel (Lemuel) not Samuel on the evil effects of intoxication (*Tale*, ll. 583 ff.). Chaucer was no doubt aware of the medieval fondness for confusing historic figures.

Naturally then in his own time, Chaucer is aware of the variability of human habits and customs. He presents the Sultana's arguments in the *Man of Law's Tale* from the Mohammedan point of view. She tells her Council of State (ll. 330 ff.) that they will suffer Hell if they deny the Koran and God's messenger, Mohammed. The scheme of her son to become a Christian will destroy them all. Here again Chaucer goes beyond his source, which by no means sees the issue from the Saracen point of view or attempts to give credibility to the deliberations of the Council. In the earlier Council meeting held by the Sultan before Constance came to Syria, his wise men saw "swich diversitee bitwene hir bothe lawes" that they could not see how he could be allowed by a Christian prince to marry his daughter (ll. 218 ff.). They were under the "lawe sweete" of Mohammed, they report. For Chaucer these Mohammedan enemies of Christianity are no silly, ignorant fools. Yet in spite of his ability to see, although not approve of, the Mohammedan point of view, Chaucer falls down on his knowledge (which was perhaps inevitable owing to the widespread ignorance concerning Islam) by assuming that Mohammedans sacrificed to God (l. 325). This is however a point of fact, not an attitude. But as we have already seen, the *Man of Law's Tale* is partially laid in the late Roman Empire and, as here, partially in the present.

In the *Squire's Tale*, we find an even broader attitude. For the Great Khan, who, we are told, subscribed to a non-Christian religion, was "*thereto* [my italics] . . . hardy, wys, and riche, / And pitous and just, alwey yliche; / Sooth of his word, benigne and honurable, / Of his corage as any centre stable" (ll. 19–22). May we not see in these lines a strong criticism of contemporary "Christian" rulers? Even the pagan can be just and kind. Chaucer's tolerance extends, later in the *Tale*, to the Khan's strange eating habits (ll. 67 ff.) and strange language (ll. 99 ff.). Yet in this tale, Chaucer substitutes space for time by presenting the distant Khan's Court in an almost Arthurian aura.

Purely from the point of view of the history of ideas, Chaucer's sense of chronology and of cultural diversity shows an affinity with certain emphases of the Renaissance.[10] In this, he draws close to Montaigne and Rabelais. And in his own time a comparison with Langland and other national contemporaries who manifest an almost total absence of such a sense brings out even more sharply the rarity of his point of view. In his century in England, I think he is paralleled in his sense of the historic only by the *Travels of Sir John Mandeville* where that sense is largely implicit rather than explicit, and by Wyclif who uses his sense of the historic for polemical purposes.

In Mandeville, we see more openly than in Chaucer, however, the workings of the scholastic concept[11] of natural reason, which is one of the roots of the modern sense of history. The great scholastics sought to demonstrate the existence of God by the light of natural reason, implanted, as they believed, in all men. The far-reaching implications of this attempt led to the belief that all men could arrive at some concept of the truth. This in turn involves the belief that to some extent at least even non-Christians have a grasp of the truth and hence other cultures are worth some consideration. If Professor R. W. Chambers was right,[12] this view lies behind More's *Utopia*.

Mandeville puts it thus:

And ye shall understand that all these men folks that have reason y[t] I have spoken of, have some articles of our faith, all if they be of divers lawes and divers beleves, yet they have some good poynts of our fayth & they beleve in God of kinde. . . .[13]

What does all this mean in terms of Chaucer's art? That is not an easy question

---

[10] I am here using the term Renaissance in the Burckhardtian sense. A. L. Rowse entitles the second chapter of his very recent *The England of Elizabeth, the Structure of Society*, 1951, pp. 31–65, "The Elizabethan Discovery of England." Chaucer can be considered a pioneer in this characteristic of the English Renaissance.

[11] The idea of natural reason and natural law goes back ultimately to Stoic speculation. But the scholastics of the thirteenth century clearly established the distinction between the knowledge gained by natural reason and that gained by faith.

[12] *Thomas More*, 1935, pp. 125 ff.

[13] Chap. CVII, Ed. Everyman's Library, p. 226.

to answer. The possession of a sense of history does not guarantee its possessor artistic powers. Yet I think we may say some things about Chaucer's art and point of view in terms of his sense of history. Like all problems dealing with the relationship between a man's views and his art, we cannot establish a strict causality.

It seems to me that through the Chaucerian sense of history, although it is only one element in the poetry of Chaucer, we may get a flavor of the essence of Chaucer's art. We see revealed in it the sense of poignancy, of the *lacrimae rerum* which often strikes any serious reader of the poet. Over much of Chaucer's work is a piercing sense of man's transience, of his foolish pretensions, of his comic-tragic dignity. The sense of the historic serves Chaucer in his satire and in his humor. It is one view which enables him to place the world in its right perspective for him—and for us. It is basic to the particular type of tragic objectivity which he often manifests. As a comic-tragic artist he makes use of a relatively new element in Western Civilization when he need not have done so. He grasped at it and made it part of his view of the world because it seemed to him, perhaps subconsciously, a way of expressing some of his most basic thoughts. It serves his artistic power of restraint. A sense of history is one of the ways Chaucer follows to enable attitudes to say themselves, to be objectified.

At the same time, as all choices must, it limits him. A comparison with Dante here will be profitable. Dante has a more profoundly tragic view than Chaucer because, in his art, he sets eternity against time. Chaucer, who in terms of religion certainly held views similar to those of Dante, rarely transferred these religious views to his art and even occasionally exhibited the scepticism of one type of believer. Much of Chaucer's art unrolls in time aware of itself through the author, the commentator

on his work. It has duration, and it conveys an awareness of this duration even as events come and go. All this will pass, Chaucer seems to say. With Dante all this has passed and is eternally judged and fixed. The actual historical events which the manifold inhabitants of hell, purgatory and heaven participated in are laid before us compassionately, but as past and as finally arbitrated. The eternal is the merciful but stern judge of history. To this stage Chaucer rarely, if ever, comes in his art. Yet his acceptance of human transitoriness and human clash of opinion and custom provides him with another spectacle from which he extracts his particular type of art. Time condemns itself and all human endeavor and hopes; and yet we cannot despair: in fact, it is only through a sense of the comic that we may fully understand dialectically our tragic dilemma. Above as within time there is need for laughter.

I do not wish to overemphasize the "modern" historical approach in Chaucer at the expense of the "medieval." In history things happen slowly. In an artistic sense, Chaucer is always modern; but he is also partially a creature of history and in him are to be seen the various conflicting ideas of the fourteenth century, some destined to wax and others to wane, perhaps only temporarily if we take a point of view long range enough. For today we may see, I think, a turning away from the historic again. But the sense of history which we find in Chaucer, however undeveloped, is one element which was destined to play a very important part in the succeeding centuries; perhaps even more important, however, it is an element which gives us some clue to the heart of the mystery of Chaucer's art. Chaucer may be studied as a figure in the history of ideas as well as an artist, and in isolating at least his sense of the historic, we must eventually turn back to his art with a new awareness and a new understanding of his aims and methods.

John Livingston Lowes

The Human Comedy

BUT Chaucer's ultimate glory is not his finished craftsmanship but the power by virtue of which he creates, through speech and action, living characters. Of his secret, as of God's—to paraphrase the drunken sapience of the Miller—it is unwise to be too inquisitive. "Goddes foyson" is there in his accomplishment, and it is enough to dwell on that.

The greatest of Chaucer's portraits within the body of a tale is the Friar in the *Summoner's Tale*, as described in the first two hundred and fifty lines or so of the narrative. I doubt if, within its compass, it has its match in English. But regarding the pilgrimage as a whole, Chaucer's masterpieces of characterization are, beyond question, the Pardoner and the Wife of Bath. Both lay bare their very selves with utter abandon—the Pardoner in a cynical disclosure, pitiless in its realism and daringly outspoken, of the hypocrisy of his preaching; the Wife of Bath (as a-moral as Falstaff and Rabelaisian before Rabelais) letting herself go with incomparable gusto and a frankness naked and unashamed, in an unexpurgated disclosure of her views upon marriage, and of her own successive marital adventures.

The Pardoner is evil to the core—the one lost soul, as Professor Kittredge once called him, among the pilgrims—with a single sharp moment of revulsion. And the tale which he tells is set as an *exemplum* in a sermon on avarice, with *radix malorum est cupiditas* as its text—a sermon rehearsed with flagrant cynicism as a taste of his qual-ity. The tale, which is one of the world's oldest and most dramatic stories of greed and death, begins, is broken in upon by the savage intensity of the sermon, then sweeps to its close with perhaps the most haunting of all personifications of Death. Then, after his instant of self-realization, the Pardoner offers, with brazen disregard of his confession, his self-discredited pardons for sale, and his callously blown-upon relics to kiss, and with crowning impudence singles out the host. And that precipitates the tensest and most repugnant moment of the journey. The whole is fearless and unsparing satire, and prologue, tale, and setting together are dramatic beyond any other unit of the Pilgrimage.

But it is the Wife of Bath who, as a figure, is the greatest of them all. In every line of her Prologue and in the whole, one feels Chaucer's delight in her creation. She is poured out, as it were, "mit einem Gusse"; she is absolutely of a piece. There is nothing else quite like her. And her superb self-revelation, with its verve and its raciness and its serenely ceaseless flow, no more to be stopped (as the Pardoner found) than the course of a planet; and above all (if Matthew Arnold's austere shade will let me apply to her the phrase which he applied to Goethe), her "profound, imperturbable naturalism"—all that is one of the few achievements which actually create a personality. John Galsworthy recently remarked, in speaking of the dramatist's tendency to fashion types instead of creating individuals: "Falstaff is perhaps the greatest excep-

Reprinted by permission of Houghton Mifflin Company and John Wilber Lowes from John Livingston Lowes, *Geoffrey Chaucer and the Development of His Genius*, Boston, 1934, pp. 229–245. This selection is Part IV of the final chapter, "The Human Comedy."

tion to this rule. We think of the gorgeous old ruffian first and last as a private person, without attaching to him any particular phase of human character." And he and that other gorgeous old sinner, the Wife of Bath, are in that respect two of a kind. They are not types; they are persons.

Even the Wife's speech has its unanalysable, individual, personal movement and turn. Wholly apart from subject-matter, you could not mistake a passage from the Pardoner's Prologue (for example) for one of hers. Every human being who possesses anything approaching personality has his own unique rhythms, tones, inflexions, build of sentences. I have a friend, a distinguished man of letters, whose expression is so individual that a single line on a post-card will unconsciously and infallibly betray his authorship. And the Eagle, Pandare, and the Wife of Bath speak like themselves and like no one else. Chaucer, who wrote for the ear, heard (I think) as he wrote, every line he put into the mouth of his characters; and of these the most individual express that unique personal quality which marks them, in the idiosyncrasies, the idiom, the very movement of their speech. Wholly apart from the sense of the words, nobody but the Wife of Bath could have uttered these lines:

> Thou seydest this, that I was lyk a cat;
> For whoso wolde senge a cattes skyn,
> Thanne wolde the cat wel dwellen in his in;
> And if the cattes skyn be slyk and gay,
> She wol nat dwelle in house half a day,
> But forth she wole, er any day be dawed,
> To shewe hir skyn, and goon a-caterwawed;
> This is to seye, if I be gay, sire shrewe,
> I wol renne out, my borel for to shewe.   D 356

Or this:

> Now wol I tellen of my fourthe
>   housbonde . . .   D 480
> By God! in erthe I was his purgatorie,
> For which I hope his soule be in
>   glorie . . .   490
> He deyde whan I cam fro Jerusalem,
> And lith ygrave under the roode-beem . . . 496

> It nys but wast to burye hym
>   preciously . . .   500
> Yet was I nevere withouten purveiance
> Of mariage, n' of othere thynges eek.
> I holde a mouses herte nat worth a leek,
> That hath but oon hole for to sterte to,
> And if that faille, thanne is al ydo.   574

Or, above all, this:

> But Lord Crist! whan that it remembereth me
> Upon my yowthe, and on my jolitee,
> It tikleth me aboute myn herte roote.
> Unto this day it dooth myn herte boote
> *That I have had my world as in my*
>   *tyme.*   D 473

The Wife of Bath was close kin to Geoffrey Chaucer. And if those last lines are not Chaucer himself to the core, then I have read the *House of Fame*, and the *Troilus*, and the greater *Tales* amiss.

And Chaucer understood her no less when he put into her mouth a cry which sums up half the passion and pain of the world:

> Allas! allas! that evere love was synne!   D 614

Nor is it out of keeping when, in the Wife's own tale of Faërye which in its ending fits her Prologue like a glove, the old hag who is a lovely lady in disguise gives an exposition of *gentilesse* which sums up the noblest thinking of the Middle Ages upon gentle breeding and true courtesy. For the Wife of Bath had a mind as keen as a sword-blade, and could rise to the height of a great argument in the dramatic realization of the lofty conception which lay at the heart of her tale. Even we occasionally have great moments.

And that lofty discourse on *gentilesse*, which owes much to Boethius and Jean de Meun, and which is steeped in Dante, raises another question. I spoke earlier of the shift of emphasis which came about between books and life, as Chaucer passed, by way of the *Troilus*, from the earlier poems to the *Canterbury Tales*—a shift whereby books passed from foreground to background, until life, rather than letters, held the stage. That is true. But half our sense of *richness*, as we read the tales, arises, whether we know it or not, from the fact that they are still saturated with the vitality and colour of Chaucer's reading. The Wife of Bath herself is not less but more Chaucer's because her speech is shot through with reminiscences of Jean de Meun and St. Jerome and Eustache Deschamps and more besides. But the elements have been distilled in Chaucer's alembic, and the result is something dreamed of by none of them—certainly not by St. Jerome! —something indefeasibly and uniquely Chaucer's own. The Wife's Prologue is not an epiphyte, but an oak, and the sap in its veins is drawn from soil enriched by the tillage of centuries.

That plausible scoundrel, the Friar in the *Summoner's Tale,* is paying his respects to the Summoner. And Chaucer again remembered Jerome's words from his diatribe against that *bête noire* of his, Jovinian: *Et tu, ille formosus monachus, crassus, nitidus, dealbatus, et quasi sponsus semper incedens* —"And thou, lovely monk, fat, shiny, bepowdered, stepping like a bridegroom." In the Friar's mouth Jerome's taunt takes on the Friar's coloration:

Me thynketh they been lyk Jovinyan,
Fat as a whale, and walkynge as a swan;
Al vinolent as botel in the spence.   D 1931

And as the passage proceeds it outdoes even St. Jerome in robustness. The exquisite humour of Madame Pertelote's diagnosis and remedies is the distillation of Chaucer's wide reading in the medical treatises of his day—a reading which enlivens other passages. The *Franklin's Tale* is enriched from his knowledge of natural magic, and the *Canon's Yeoman's Tale* from his conversance with alchemical treatises, and the *Wife of Bath's Tale* from his absorption in Dante's great discourse on *nobiltà* in the *Convivio.* And constantly, as he writes, his memory flashes back and forth among his books, and his recollections, with colours caught from their sojourn in his mind, are woven into the texture of the tales. Scholars have sedulously gathered them up and listed them, and the lists *per se* are as dead and as desiccated as herbariums. In their context they are alive. For the *zest* of Chaucer's reading communicates itself to his recollections, and his learning is permeated with his authentic personal quality. And in different moods different tracts of his reading come back to memory. When he is deeply moved he is apt to remember Dante, and particularly that passage in which Dante, too, was most profoundly stirred—the sublime prayer of St. Bernard to Mary with which the last canto of the *Paradiso* opens. It is with one of Dante's majestic invocations that the *Troilus* closes, and, blended with reminiscences of the Bible and of the great hymns from the Service of the Church, St. Bernard's prayer again lends grave beauty to the Prologues of the Prioress and the Second Nun. Or, *per contra,* some staid and erudite passage will be touched with mischievous humour, as if it had been dipped in some impish wizard's converting spring—as when Chauntecleer gravely translates for Madame Pertelote a scrap of monkish Latin which in *Melibeus* Chaucer had rendered with perfect propriety:

For al so siker as *In principio,*
Mulier est hominis confusio,—
Madame, the sentence of this Latyn is,
"Womman is mannes joye and al his
      blis."   B 4356

Learning could not live long in Chaucer's mind without assimilation to the temper of that bright spirit.

And the reason, at least in part, is not far to seek. Professor Garrod, who has the trick of setting down penetrating critical judgments with the engaging air of making casual remarks, once said of Matthew Arnold: "He thinks too much of the uses of literature, and too little of its pleasures. He attaches too much importance to taste, and too little to *relish.*" That last is one of the reasons why Matthew Arnold never really understood Chaucer. For I can think of no other poet—Shakespeare being always *hors concours*—who brought to both books and life such relish and whose work is so instinct with zest. Some of the old voyagers had it, and Dampier's description of *hocshu*, and Oviedo's of the coconut, have a gusto not unworthy of Chaucer. Even he, I think, never surpassed in its kind his initial description of the Canon's Yeoman, as by hard riding he overtakes the pilgrims at Boghton under Blee. For never elsewhere has a hot and sweating human being been metamorphosed with such delectation into a masterpiece.

His hakeney, that was al pomely grys,
So swatte, that it wonder was to
   see . . .   G 560
The hors eek that his yeman rood upon
So swatte, that unnethe myghte it gon.
Aboute the peytrel stood the foom ful hye,
He was of foom al flekked as a pye . . .   565
A clote-leef he hadde under his hood
For swoot, and for to keep his heed from heete.
But it was joye for to seen hym swete!
His forheed dropped as a stillatorie.   579

If ever the Terentian *nihil humanum* was exemplified, it is there! The Canon's Yeoman sweat magnificently, gloriously; it was like looking on one of Nature's wonders to observe him. And Chaucer's individual, peculiar quality lies in large measure in that eager appetence of his for life, to which nothing was common or unclean. One meets it everywhere. The Wife of Bath is talking about her gay gowns, which she wore (especially when her fourth husband was safely away in London) to vigils and processions and preachings and plays and marriages. Then, she says,

[I] wered upon my gaye scarlet gytes.
Thise wormes, ne thise motthes, ne thise mytes,
Upon my peril, frete hem never a deel.   D 561

The relish in that twice repeated "thise," with its ineffable familiarity, is beyond words. "Worms, moths, and mites" are simply worms, moths, and mites—only

that, and nothing more. "*Thise* wormes, *thise* motthes, *thise* mytes" have become intimates—brothers and sisters, like (with a difference!) St. Francis' "our brother, the wind, and our sister water." And the same graphic immediacy of conception in another passage vividly anthropomorphizes God. Prayers, says that affable arch-hypocrite the Summoner's Friar,—"prayeres"

Of charitable and chaste bisy freres
Maken hir sours [flight] to *Goddes eres*
   two.   D 1941

The *ear* of God is little more than an abstraction—"Neither [is] his ear heavy, that it cannot hear." "God's *two ears*" startlingly visualizes, humanizes God. And the daring familiarity which the Friar allows himself is not only an apt touch in a masterpiece of satirical portraiture but also, once more, an instance of Chaucer's imaginative coalescence with his subject.

Moreover, every passage which, for other ends, I have quoted in this section brings sharply before us a kindred quality of Chaucer's mind—his instinct for the concrete. "Thou seydest this, that I was lyk a cat"; "I holde a mouses herte nat worth a leek, That hath but oon hole for to sterte to"; "It tikleth me aboute myn herte roote"; "Fat at a whale . . . walkynge as a swan . . . vinolent as botel in the spence"; "Siker as *In principio*"; a sweating dapple-gray horse flecked with foam like a magpie; a burdock-leaf under a hood; a forehead dropping sweat like a still; worms, moths, and mites, and scarlet gowns; God's two ears. "You poets," Landor makes Porson say in one of the *Imaginary Conversations*—"you poets are still rather too fond of the unsubstantial. Some will have nothing else than what they call pure imagination. . . . *I hate both poetry and wine without body.*" On that score Chaucer's withers are unwrung! In a master's hand and in its place the concrete carries straight and true to the mark, as Dante, Villon, Bunyon, Defoe all knew, and none better than the writers of the great Biblical narratives. Turn to the stories of Jacob, or Joseph, or Moses, or Deborah, or to the closing chapters of the Book of Job, or the accounts of the betrayal in the garden, or the Revelation of St. John, and see what their vividness owes to concrete detail. Or re-read *Les regrets de la belle Heaulmière*, or *The Pilgrim's Progress*, or *Robinson Crusoe*. Then come back, for a new sense of their mastery, to the great tales in which Chaucer has a free hand.

Here, for example, are the lines in which the Reeve unexpectedly unlocks his heart:

Yet in oure asshen olde is fyr
   yreke . . .   A 3882
Oure olde lemes mowe wel been unweelde,
But wyl ne shal nat faillen, that is sooth.
And yet ik have alwey a coltes tooth,
As many a yeer as it is passed henne
Syn that my tappe of lif bigan to renne.
For sikerly, whan I was bore, anon
Deeth drough the tappe of lyf and leet it gon;
And ever sithe hath so the tappe yronne,
Til that almoost al empty is the tonne.
The streem of lyf now droppeth on the
   chymbe.   3896

And here, in the Pardoner's exposure of his homiletic tricks, is a picture so telling in its concrete realization of bodily action that one not only visualizes the movements but feels one's self incipiently reproducing them:

Thanne peyne I me to strecche forth the nekke,
And est and west upon the peple I bekke,
As dooth a dowve sittynge on a berne.
Myne handes and my tonge goon so yerne,
That it is joye to se my bisynesse—   C 399

as it was joy to see the Canon's Yeoman sweat! Relish and the concreteness which Landor called "body," in Chaucer go hand in hand.

For as Milton's archangel's sky-tinctured wings were of colours dipt in heaven, the great Tales, as Chaucer tells them, are not merely dipt, but drenched, in life. And characters which came to him lay figures became in speech and action more vividly alive than most of us. Even a cock and hen,

which he had found plain cock and hen, have become, without for a moment ceasing to be fowls, vivaciously and captivatingly human. Read the story of the *Nun's Priest's Tale* in any older version—beast fable or beast epic as you will—and see what Chaucer has done. And then, to see what Chaucer alone can do, read line by line with it the retelling of the tale by even so great a poet and master of the vernacular as Dryden.

Pekke hem up right as they growe and ete hem
   yn.
Be myrie, housbonde, for youre fader
   kyn!   B 4158

That is Chaucer. Now John Dryden:

Eat these, and be, my lord, of better cheer;
Your father's son was never born to fear.

Or Chaucer again:

Madame Pertelote, my worldes blis,
Herkneth thise blisful briddes how they synge,
And se the fresshe floures how they
   sprynge.   B 4392

Then Dryden once more:

Then turning, said to Partlet: 'See, my dear,
How lavish nature has adorn'd the year;
How the pale primrose and blue violet spring,
And birds essay their throats disus'd to sing.

Whatever Chaucer touched, when what Byron called the *estro* was upon him, has a zest, a spontaneity, a raciness, which are inimitable and unique. The specific difference of the *Canterbury Tales* is their immersion in *life*—which is tantamount to saying (to amend my metaphor) that they are dipt in Geoffrey Chaucer.

Mutatis mutandis, that is true of his verse. And again I have the masterpieces especially in mind. For verse which retains the qualities of living speech—its turns, inflexions, stresses, *nuances*, which are its body, as we may call the incorporated sense its soul—such verse Chaucer wrote as few have ever written it. Here are three stanzas only of the swift, light touch-and-go of the dialogue between Pandare and Criseyde as the Second Book of the *Troilus* begins:

"As evere thryve I," quod this Pandarus,
"Yet koude I telle a thyng to doon you pleye."
"Now, uncle deere," quod she, "telle it us
For Goddes love; is than th' assege aweye?
I am of Grekes so fered that I deye."
"Nay, nay," quod he, "as evere mote I thryve!
It is a thing wel bet than swyche fyve."

"Ye, holy God!" quod she, "what thyng is that?
What! bet than swyche fyve? I! nay, ywys!
For al this world ne kan I reden what
It sholde ben; som jape, I trowe, is this;
And but youreselven telle us what it is,
My wit is for t'arede it al to leene;
As help me God, I not nat what ye meene."

"And I youre borugh, ne nevere shal, for me,
This thyng be told to yow, as mote I thryve!"
"And whi so, uncle myn? whi so?" quod she.
"By God," quod he, "that wol I telle as blyve!
For proudder womman is ther noon on lyve,
And ye it wist, in al the town of Troye;
I jape nought, as evere have I joye!"   II, 140

The verse, flawlessly metrical, weaves itself through and around the light-hearted, gaily colloquial, irresponsible chatter, without an instant's check to its sparkling flow. And the dialogue in the *Summoner's Tale* between the Friar and the sick man Thomas and Thomas's wife is unmatched for its revelation of character, not only through the meanings which words convey, but also through the very cast of the suave, unctuous, hypocritical sentences. No one who reads with ear as well as eye—and an ear no less than an eye is a *sine qua non* for the reading of Chaucer—can fail to catch the subtly characterized inflexions of the Friar's voice. Read as Chaucer's contemporaries read it, there is no such body of flexible, musical narrative verse as his in English—and none (at its best) so superbly forthright and direct.

Finally, I am not greatly concerned about Chaucer's alleged defect of "the σπουδαιό-της, the high and excellent seriousness, which Aristotle assigns as one of the grand virtues of poetry." The poet who wrote the closing stanzas of the *Troilus*, and the Invocation to the Virgin in the Prologue of the Second Nun, and the Prioress's Prologue and Tale, and the noble balade *Truth*; whose memory was enriched from the wisdom of Boethius and the Bible; who was moved by the beauty of the hymns and the service of the Church, and who turned at will to the sublimest cantos of the *Purgatorio* and the *Paradiso*—that poet was not deficient in seriousness, high or deep. He had, to be sure, no "message." But his sanity ("He is," said Dryden, "a perpetual fountain of good sense"), his soundness, his freedom from sentimentality, his balance of humorous detachment and directness of vision, and above all his large humanity—those are qualities which "give us," to apply Arnold's own criterion, "what we can rest upon." And we should be hard put to it to name another poet with clearer title to rank with those who, in Philip Sidney's words, "teach by a divine delightfulness."